SECRETS FROM THE DELPHI CAFÉ

UNLOCKING
THE CODE TO HAPPINESS

Scott Friedman & Bob Rich

with Mike Pehanich

06 07 08 09 10 HH 5 4 3 2 1
First Edition
Printed in the United States of America
ISBN 10: 0-9778811-0-5
ISBN 13: 978-0-9778811-0-9
SEL016000 Self-Help/Personal Growth/Happiness
Library of Congress Control Number: 2006922458

$17.95 U.S. Funds

For additional information or to request permission to make copies of any part of this work please contact: Scott Friedman at 716-853-5100 or email sfriedman@lippes.com

We gratefully dedicate this book to our wives and to our children:

Lisa	*Mindy*
Samantha	*Kim*
Eliza	*Bob*
Julia	*Ted*
Madeline	*Barney*

Acknowledgements

Scott would like to acknowledge Dr. Dan Baker, Director of Canyon Ranch's Life Enhancement Center, for his friendship and for sharing his insights over the years, particularly with respect to his work in the new field of positive psychology. We would also like to thank Samantha Friedman for creating the concept for our book's cover.

Just as family plays a major role in *Secrets*, we recognize the part our families have played in our own efforts to unlock the code to happiness.

We consider ourselves fortunate to have fathers who, while following different pursuits, have served as wonderful role models. Irwin Friedman is a well-recognized and compassionate physician; Bob Rich, Sr. was a hard-driving entrepreneur. Both fathers always made time to mentor us and other young professionals in their respective fields, and we are indebted to them for their wise advice over the years.

We also consider ourselves fortunate to have had great role models in our mothers, Iris Friedman and Janet Rich, to whom, along with our fathers, we are indebted for their many lessons in love, compassion, and patience.

Children can be a great source of wisdom, and we learn as much from our children every day as they learn from us. We appreciate the excitement with which they have shared our journey.

Finally, our wives and best friends, Lisa and Mindy, have done so much more than patiently read manuscripts and offer great feedback. Their ideas have merged with our own throughout the text, and we consider them equal partners in this project.

"IF WE LIVE GOOD LIVES, THE TIMES ARE ALSO GOOD.
AS WE ARE, SUCH ARE THE TIMES."

ST. AUGUSTINE

Contents

INTRODUCTION

This is a book about happiness. Perhaps more accurately, it is a book about finding increased opportunities to savor life's abundant blessings and, when necessary, to more skillfully manage the inevitable challenges each of us face, including the realities of sickness, death, pain, cruelty, injustice or just plain disappointment.

The content of this book is the culmination of more than thirty years of retrospection and conversation with my friend, Bob Rich. I first met Bob when we were paired against each other in a local tennis tournament. I was a junior in high school, and he was president of one of our city's largest companies. My only focus that day was to try to take advantage of our roughly fifteen year age difference by outrunning and outlasting Bob in our match.

To this day, I don't remember who won the match, but I'll always cherish the friendship that we started that afternoon, sitting courtside in sweaty clothes and talking about sports, school, business, and even a little bit about life in general.

Although, between starting a family and a career as a lawyer, I found less and less time to play tennis, I did manage to stay in touch with Bob. A relationship that began as a competition on a playing field somehow evolved over the years from opponent, to mentor, to friend and, now, co-author. While I am delighted to have had the chance to write this book with Bob, it will always be his friendship that I cherish most.

Our friendship developed over the years, as we came together for periodic chats about our families and relationships as well as our businesses, but which would, typically, turn to broader issues, including life, death, success, and happiness. Sometimes our discussions were narrowly framed by the particular events we were living through; other times we would discuss insights and lessons from civilization's great religions or philosophies; still other times we'd talk about bestselling books or articles we'd seen in popular magazines and newspapers.

One day we were chatting, and I suggested we draw on some of our discussions and experiences over the years, as well as the lessons we had internalized from great religions, philosophies and thinkers, and co-author a book on happiness, a subject on which we've reflected since some of our earliest courtside chats.

To help explore this subject more thoughtfully, as we began to organize our thoughts, we broadened our conversation to include Mike Pehanich, a writer and philosopher. Mike's suggestions were invaluable as we framed our thoughts and our story. In addition, Mike's assistance with the writing of this book enhanced it immeasurably. Our book would not be the same without his contributions.

We decided to create a fictional character, Socrates Smith, who embarks on a mystical journey of self-awareness. To make the lessons Smith learns on his journey – the very lessons Bob and I internalized from our conversations over the years – clearer, more memorable, and more easily integrated into your own life, we created a "Code to Happiness" which Smith discovers in the course of his journey.

We encourage you to test our Code and judge for yourself whether this approach really works. We hope that our story and Code will have great relevance and meaning to you, no matter what your age or background. Most importantly, we hope that our story of Socrates Smith will help you to continue to discover and follow your own path to living a happy, fulfilling life!

- Scott

CHAPTER ONE

THE DREAM

Call me Socrates Smith. It's not my birth name. I've more or less inherited it. It came to me in a strange dream – a dream born of a meeting and a reading and the hand of Fate.

I t all started with a cup of coffee.

Every morning I go to the DΣLPHI Café for a cup o' joe and some time to think before I hit the office. The lunches are good. The breakfasts are better. The coffee is superb.

I always exchange a few words with the waitress, Sophie, before I settle in with my newspaper and my thoughts. Sophie looks a lot like a young Cher. Seems to know everything. She never went to college, and, as far as anyone knows, never ran a business other than the DΣLPHI's breakfast business. But she appears to know every man and woman on the street, and all the daily news from the headlines to the sports pages.

And a lot about people.

The DΣLPHI is the kind of sanctuary that everyone should have – a friendly, peaceful place where you can get your head together before you get back on the fast track or the slow track or whatever track suits your pace. You can see and feel the grain and scars of the heavy hardwood tables and smell the coffee that George Niketopoulous keeps in ready supply – his special house blend and two exotic flavors every morning. With Sophie working the counter, you never see the bottom of your mug. You can read the paper or a book, work a crossword, plan your day, or just sip and think without a worry and only a rare interruption.

So there I was, soberly assessing the turns my life had taken recently. The worst situation was Dad. His health had gone south again, dimming the hope we had felt a month ago when his cancer seemed to have gone into remission. All we could do now was keep his hopes – and our own – afloat.

Things weren't looking good at the office either. After five straight quarters of missed projections, heads were about to roll.

And the kids. I came to believe a long time ago that even "good" kids give their parents gray hairs. I have three *great* kids, but they offer their own brand of challenges. My oldest is Ellen. She will be graduating college with honors this year. I'd rather she were graduating with high hopes. Ellen can't seem to shake that dark cloud of pessimism and self-doubt. I still hoped that college would teach her how to smile before she graduated.

Then there's Randy, the rock star in waiting. What a character! God, how I love his energy and spirit! But, oh, how I hate his music. Well, maybe not all of it. And maybe "hate" is the wrong word. It's hard to hate something your kid lives for. Most of the time when I hear his music, all I can do is silently pray that he finishes soon. Yet every once in a while, I will hear a beat or a ballad that makes me realize there's soul or talent beneath those hypnotic rhythms and blaring bass. Yeah, I'd feel a lot more comfortable if he directed some of that passion toward a career with a future. I am a parent, after all, and worry about the road of dreams he is taking.

Eddie is our youngest. A teenager. Need I say more? He really keeps us on our toes. Watching him and his pals is one revelation after another. I know parents whose kids seem to get nothing lower than an A-. Not Eddie. We're happy with a steady stream of Bs and Cs because, on occasion, even those grades seem hard to come by. But what a quarterback! Maybe football will be his ticket to college. Only time will tell.

I sipped my coffee. My mind floated back and forth between thoughts of family and friends, Dad, and my job. Who ever knows what strange turns life will take, no matter what road you choose and no matter how well you plan. Lord knows, I've sure deviated from my roadmap a time or two, especially after my first wife died. Pain? Disappointment? Loss? You can't walk through life without bumping into them. But, looking at the big picture, I can't complain. I have a great family and a lot of friends. I remarried several years ago. My wife Carrie has been a loving – a wonderful – stepmother to the kids.

A familiar voice interrupted my reverie.

"Whose flower is that?" Before I could look up, Sophie had filled my cup.

"It's yours, Sophie," I said, and she swept up the loose bargain rose I had bought from a gap-toothed guy at the stoplight that morning. I enjoy an opportunity to spread a little cheer.

Sophie broke the stem, and slipped the rose into the sweep of brunette around her right ear.

"Thanks," she said. "Any special occasion this time?"

"Just my appreciation for keeping the mug full," I answered.

She smiled at me and turned to take care of another customer. I watched her glide gracefully through the café. The rose nestled in her hair gave her a gypsy's air that only added to her mystique.

The café filled rapidly with its mix of regulars and drop-ins. Many of the DΣLPHI faithful I knew by name or reputation, compliments of Sophie. What an interesting cross-section of humanity! I recognized the man at the counter, talking to George Niketopoulous. His name was Phillip Stover, a cheerful man who owned several very successful businesses, including a prominent software firm. He had headed numerous civic projects and charitable causes over the years. He was one of the city's go-to guys. He always delivered.

The drop-ins seemed equally interesting. A man in a tightly fastened khaki trench coat looked like Humphrey Bogart. I had seen him several times at the DΣLPHI. He seemed to have some of Bogart's mannerisms, too. I recognized a few of the well-known businessmen and women, a pair of lawyers, and several others whom I didn't know but whose faces I recognized as DΣLPHI regulars. A tall, black-haired woman, who seemed curt and circumspect, reached into her purse and paid her bill. She had a mysterious Eastern European air about her.

"There are a million stories in the Naked City," said Sophie, taking me by surprise.

"That was one of my dad's lines," I said, yielding elbowroom to her coffee pot.

"They've all got a story to tell," she said, panning the room, the untold stories of the DΣLPHI's patrons flickering behind her dark eyes.

My father had copped the "Naked City" line from a popular TV show during my youth, and he dropped it in a mischievous manner on my mother, relatives, or anyone sucked into knee-deep gossip. But now the phrase meant something else, and it stirred a rush of curiosity as I glanced around the DΣLPHI.

"I wonder, Sophie," I began, pausing for a moment to consider my question. "Who, from this distinguished cross-section of humanity, would you guess is the happiest person in here?" I asked.

She looked curiously at me for a moment before responding. "You could be," she said, adjusting the rose as if it were a cherished accessory.

"Thanks," I said. "But I doubt your more distinguished clientele would care to switch places with me."

Then a different look came into her eye, one I had witnessed on a handful of occasions...right before she bowled you over with a remark.

"No," she said. "I said *you could be*. In fact, you could be the happiest person in the world." She leaned over the table, locked me with her brown eyes, and let her words settle in. Her look beckoned me. Toward what, I could not say. Her entreaty was a call to something that, at the moment, I couldn't begin to grasp.

As Sophie left to take an order, an urge began to peck at my brain cells, working them over like a flock of pigeons devouring a spilled bag of popcorn. Surely, I was better off than many, not as fortunate as others. But the subject was happiness, not financial success. Who, I wondered, was the happiest person in the DΣLPHI? Who, for that matter, was the happiest person in the world? What a prize you would have if you could tap his – or her – secret! Wasn't happiness everyone's Holy Grail? Wasn't happiness the ultimate reward?

The questions raced through my head as I finished my coffee with a long swallow and headed for the door.

◇◇◇◇

Nearly 2500 years ago, Socrates declared that "the unexamined life is not worth living," and I guess I would have to agree. I had studied a little philosophy in college and had examined my life and the lives around me about as much as anyone I knew. In the wake of Sophie's strange pronouncement, a philosophical challenge now buoyed me.

Happiness.

It was one of those capital letter pursuits ranked up there with Truth and Knowledge. Even with my kids and their friends, I bet that it stood right up there with "popularity," "good looks," and a new set of wheels. Rich or poor, famous or unknown, it didn't matter. Happiness was everyone's goal.

Many of the great minds had pondered happiness. Indeed, Aristotle had said that "Happiness is the meaning and the purpose of life, the whole aim and end of human existence." Great Eastern philosophers, like Confucius, also had pondered the secrets to happiness in their own traditions. Their meanings and paths to happiness might differ, but at least one thing was clear: *happiness* was much more than wearing a "happy face." Neither was it as simple as a mindless pursuit of "good times" or weekend distraction from work week challenges. Instead, the great minds all found happiness inextricably linked to living a good life. An authentic life. One that you could feel satisfied with, at any point along the journey. It was that simple. And that complex.

The more I thought about it, the more intrigued I became. I was starting to feel like a bloodhound about to be set loose on a hot trail, ready to put my nose to the hunt. Who was the happiest person in town? And what was his or her secret?

I walked the last block to the office and settled into work. About mid-morning, I stretched and headed to the coffee station.

"Smitty," I heard my boss, Phil, yell as I passed his office. "Got a minute?"

"What's up?"

"Close the door," he said ominously. Phil's one of those One-Minute Manager types who always keeps in touch, engages you, and knows what you are doing without looking over your shoulder too much. He keeps meetings short – one of his most endearing qualities, folks around the office will tell you. So a little red flag waved across my mind when he said: "Sit down. We need to talk."

I settled into a high-back leather chair designed for comfort with the foreboding that what Phil had to say would be anything but comforting. The worry lines had made a topographical map of Phil's face.

"Boy, that's a telling look," I said. "Who got the axe?"

"You'll need a long scorecard," said Phil. He was hunched over, his shoulders sloping from an unseen burden. "A downsizing mandate. They've ordered a 20 percent cut. Across the board. From the mailroom to the executive suite. Even one of our most valuable strategic planners is getting cut," he said, his eyes now unable to look at mine.

"Is anything negotiable?"

"Probably not. It's Friday. They are planning to make the public announcement this afternoon."

"Great news for the guys to take home to their families. They'll have all weekend to celebrate," I said wryly.

"I just thought I should tell you." Phil rubbed his hand across his thinning hair. "I'm sorry. I don't know how they think we're gonna turn this ship around when we get rid of some of our best people!" His voice trailed off for a moment.

"Especially a guy like you…with your smarts, your service…But you're top drawer, Smitty. You're known and respected in the industry. I'm sure you'll have no problem finding work."

I looked at Phil without saying a word. I felt a mix of fear and anger in the pit of my stomach. Easy for my still-employed boss to feel so confident.

I ignored the flattery and asked, "What's the severance package?" I had a bad feeling about what was coming.

"Two weeks for most. Something more for guys like you. It's still being worked out."

"That's great. I can't wait to find out." We shook hands, and I walked out the door.

So much for *happiness*.

The health club was packed. The noon rush was worse than usual. I had to cut my workout short, so I ran a couple of hard miles, rapped the speed bag, and pummeled the heavy bag until the sweat poured down in buckets. A short stretch and cool down, and that was it for the day.

The official word on termination came that afternoon. We were called en masse to the cafeteria where they explained the company's decision. Phil quietly gave me an envelope that disclosed I had been given two months severance. One of the largest packages awarded, Phil told me. Hooray for small victories.

I tried to settle several of the shell-shocked victims with words of encouragement. But it was Black Friday, and few were ready to be consoled. Handshakes. Perfunctory whispers of mutiny among some survivors. And then, mercifully, we parted amid a flood of fond farewells and pledges to stay in touch. I went back to my office to tie up a few loose ends. Pride, habit, and gratitude prodded me to make a handful of phone calls to associates I needed to thank and say good-bye to. When I was finished, I sent an e-mail with my latest draft of the department's business plan to the others in my group who would remain on.

Then I turned off my company computer for the last time.

A note from my wife, Carrie, awaited me on the kitchen table. Dad had called. He was feeling "punk" again. It was a term I associated with my youth. "What's the matter, kid? Feeling punk today?" he would say to a son hot with fever, rubbing my hair and cupping my cheek in gentle support.

His hands, I believed, had the power to heal.

Every one of his visits to the doctor filled our family with dread. We were not sure how much longer he could battle the cancer that had returned a few months ago. We were on unfamiliar ground. His reassuring words were hard to hold on to. I wondered how bad Dad really felt if he admitted to feeling punk. He rarely complained about anything.

Carrie arrived a few minutes later. I tried to brace her for the day's news. The double blow of losing my job and Dad's condition hit her hard, but she tried to remain strong and show her support.

Our conversation toggled back and forth between Dad's illness and my job-lessness.

Carrie had lost her mother little more than a year ago, so the prospect of facing another family loss weighed down her usually buoyant spirit. As for my layoff, I tried to be optimistic. I had a good reputation and felt I'd land on my feet soon. But our financial situation scared Carrie. There was no hiding that. She herself had taken on an office job to help out with family finances less than two years before. But she was still new to the workforce after long years at home, and she had only a small salary and little marketable experience to show for her efforts to date. My loving wife could only parrot my frequent response to challenges and mishaps.

"Well, you've always said that change is opportunity," she said stoically. "Let's see what kind of opportunity this one brings."

That evening in my library, before the weight of the day's events had settled, I thumbed through the volumes on my bookshelves. It was an eclectic assortment of books accumulated over several decades, and I treated them reverently. But now I perused them with special – almost guided – purpose. I needed some flash of insight, a gulp of understanding. Certainly the great minds had something of value for occasions like this – words of wisdom, perspective…something better than a stiff drink, at least. I thought of my earlier discussion with Sophie on happiness and wondered what the great minds had written on the subject.

I opened "The Apology of Socrates" by Plato. I read swiftly at first, and then slowed to savor my favorite part, the section in which the Delphic Oracle proclaims that no man is wiser than Socrates. Socrates refuses to believe the oracle, and he travels throughout Greece in search of a wiser man than he to satisfy his doubt. His frustrating, illuminating hunt draws resentment from the many proud but not-so-wise men whose ignorance Socrates unveils during the course of his earnest inquiry. Finally, Socrates yields to the oracle's judgment that he is, indeed, the wisest of men, for he alone grasps the limits of his understanding in his timeless quest.

I had read the book before, but never with such pleasure and avid interest. It was nearly midnight when I closed the book. The last lines of Socrates resonated in the silence of my study.

"Now it is time we were going, I to die and you to live; but which of us has the happier prospect is unknown to anyone but God."

There was that simple root word once again – happy – present in Socrates' very last sentence to his executioners before drinking a fatal dose of hemlock.

The house was wonderfully quiet. I brushed my teeth, made my rounds. I checked in on Randy and Eddie, found Carrie fast asleep. I thought to call Ellen, but I did not wish to disturb a college kid's slumber, though I sometimes wondered if she slept at all. I sat down in my favorite chair and stared out into the darkened sky. I was a lucky man. I had a lot to be grateful for. My mind flickered with thoughts of Socrates and my dad. I hoped that I would always live bravely like both of them. Brave in life. Brave in the face of death. Maybe I wasn't the happiest man around, but all things considered, I felt like a fortunate man. A lucky guy, indeed.

A curious crowd had gathered around me. I was puzzled. Why were they dressed in robes and tunics? Why was I, for that matter? We ambled along the stone road deep in discussion. Though I could not place them, many faces in the crowd seemed quite familiar. Oddly, all waited to hear from me.

"Living well and justly are the same thing." Had the words come from me? The crowd listened earnestly. An oration followed, my thoughts earnest but muddled.

The crowd dissolved, and I found myself locked in dialogue with a man in a fine white tunic. Its red trim marked him as a man of distinction. Our topic was happiness, and I asked the man what it was, if he had attained it, and how his life was better as a result. But he grew increasingly perturbed as we spoke, barking at servants, interrupting our discussion to send messages regarding his enterprises. That he had accumulated considerable wealth and power was certain. But, with his chronic worry and peevishness, he hardly seemed to be a happy man.

On and on the dream revolved, with animated discussions with my companions on the stone streets of Athens alternating with unconvincing, sober monologues from men in elegant robes who could not say enough about their own success, knowledge, or wealth. They had everything – everything, that is, except what I sought.

But among some, both rich and poor, I began to see flashes of light. Yes, there were men among us of both great and modest means who seemed to have pieces of what everyone pursued. Some became discouraged when I could not give them more and better answers, and they soon left our ranks. But others hung on, asking more questions, sharing their thoughts. Their pleasure and hope grew with each step.

Next, I found myself in a large room of cut stone and marble. Burning lamps lit its dark corners.

One of the lamps grew with blinding light, and out of its brilliance emerged a form. A beautiful woman in a white robe suddenly stood before me. She possessed bold features, flashing eyes, and high-arching eyebrows. A red rose was nestled in her hair.

A voice resonated through the temple.

"Is anyone happier than Socrates Smith?"

"No one," said the woman.

And as I awoke from the dream, I heard her voice again.

"No one."

I drifted between that blissful state and an awakening world with the sounds of our household coming to life. For several minutes, I hovered in that limbo, not sure which alley of consciousness to enter. Reality took hold when Eddie's flat feet slapped on our wooden floor. Carrie clanged the breakfast dishes. Randy blared some nondescript tune in search of sane lyrics through the hiss of the shower. I had overslept, but, pulsing with the excitement of the oracle's words, I was glad I had.

I dressed quickly, kissed Carrie, and headed for the door.

"Where are you off to in such a hurry?" she asked. "Did you forget that it's Saturday?"

"I have an appointment," I said.

"A job appointment?"

"Not exactly."

"With whom?" She seemed a little disappointed.

"With an oracle."

And I rushed out the door.

The DƐLPHI was hopping with its weekend crowd. Most of the faces looked new, and more talk than thought filled the café. George rang the register like a soulful musician.

I grabbed a newspaper but felt little desire to read. I held a cup between two hands and felt the sting of hot coffee on my lips.

"I knew you'd be back," said a voice. And there stood Sophie as bright as the cosmic flame I had witnessed in my morning dream.

I tried not to act surprised. Failed.

"How did you know? I'm rarely here on Saturday," I mumbled.

"You need something," she said, filling my cup.

"What's that?"

"The Code."

"A code?"

"No, *the* Code," she corrected with a welcoming nod. "The Code to Happiness!"

CHAPTER TWO

THE FISHERMAN

She was gone before I could coax another syllable out of her.

A code…No, *the* Code, she had corrected. Oh, yeah. *The Code*. Sure! What was I thinking?

I had no idea what she was talking about. Sophie floated from table to table, topping off coffee mugs with her usual charm and chatter. She stopped momentarily to speak with the businessman, Philip Stover. I watched Stover grow serious, his eyes tight and focused as he listened to her half-whispered words above the Saturday morning din of the DΣLPHI. I wondered what revelations this captivating woman had for him. Town gossip had it that Phillip's business acumen bordered on the supernatural. Was Sophie the source behind his genius for wealth? Their exchange seemed to grow more serious and secretive. I couldn't help but stare at them. Sophie caught my eye. I turned away, somewhat embarrassed. Seconds later, I heard them both laughing.

I returned to my morning paper, sipping my coffee while waiting for a chance to speak with Sophie. She seemed particularly busy, however, and by the time I was through skimming the paper, we still hadn't spoken. Oh, well. Maybe best to catch her another day. I stood up, ready to head out into the beckoning sunshine.

"Where are you going so quickly?" said Sophie, over my left shoulder.

Turning, I looked at her but didn't answer.

"So? Are you ready to go to work?" Her dark eyes fixed on me suddenly, barely a foot away. "Socrates Smith."

I sat again, stunned. Where had she heard that moniker? It had been my dream, not hers. I was almost too astonished to respond.

"OK. Clue me in." I said, trying to compose myself. Was I on to something important or simply the target of a grand hoax?

"I mean, am I supposed to believe that there's a secret Code to Happiness? I heard you and Stover laughing."

"Oh, yes. Happiness is no laughing matter. Someone is always conniving and plotting to take it from us. They'll even laugh at us to take it away!" she said, dripping in sarcasm as she wiped the table. "It's amazing, isn't it? Happiness is almost in our grasp, right before our eyes, waiting to sweep us away. But people and circumstances and obligations keep messing it up, don't they? It's a great conspiracy to make us miserable. To rob us of our day in the sun."

The mix of her smile and sarcasm disarmed me. "OK. I think I get your point," I said, unable to hold back a smile.

Sophie laughed. "Listen, Mr. Smith. Hang your skepticism on the hat rack and leave it there. Trust me. You've got great potential."

"Why's that?" I said.

Sophie just rolled her eyes. "Cynical doesn't become you, Smith" she said, setting down her dish rag and leaning on her palms. "You're not the first person who's stared lifelong happiness in the face but couldn't take the first step to seize it."

"First step, nothing! This whole thing has me a little spooked," I said. "Tell me, what is the first step on the road – I mean, the code – to happiness?"

Sophie became suddenly serious. Her eyes seemed to penetrate to the depths of my soul. She sensed what I needed and what I had. I wasn't sure what to expect. What could she say that would forever unlock the secrets of happiness?

Instead, she left me hanging..

"Be patient," she advised. "Life has a way of revealing the code to those who are open to it. It will come…in due time." She turned and walked away to help another customer.

That was it. I got up and paid my bill, holding back my impatience and disappointment. What was I expecting?

"Smitha, my frien', how are you?" George Niketopoulous said with that heavy Greek accent that decades in America had not tempered. The ends of his moustache met the contours of his cheeks.

"I'm fine, George," I said. "I'll take a cup to go."

"My coffee is the best, yes?"

Sophie disappeared into the kitchen.

"The best, George. You serve only the best."

Again, vivid dreams filled my night. So clear and palpable were the figures that appeared and guided my way that I cannot judge them less real than those that surround me as I compose these pages.

This time, I was sitting on a big rock next to my father, watching our lines and waiting for the fish to bite. The setting sun was spectacular. I struggled to discern my father's words, but they were muffled and I could not make them out. A warbling sound intruded upon his words. The sound broke, returned. I shook myself awake and found myself in my own bed.

This time the ring was clear and demanding. I reached across Carrie's quiet body and grabbed the phone from the bed stand. The broken numerals of the alarm clock read 5:00.

"H-hallo," I growled like a bear awakened from hibernation. Silence.

"Dad?"

It was Ellen. I had never grown entirely accustomed to her calls at ungodly hours, usually between midnight and 6:00 AM.

"Yes, Honey. It's me."

"Did I wake you?"

"That's OK. Had to get up soon anyway." I nervously wondered to myself if she was alright and why she had called. "How are you doing?" I asked.

"Not so well." Another pause and then she launched into a litany of concerns, none of which struck me as terribly important or troublesome in my still dazed state. I listened patiently. After we hung up half an hour later, I found myself wondering whether my comments had done any good. I wasn't optimistic. Her depression was hard to figure. Ellen's scholastic record was the stuff of a proud parent's dreams. Our walls were filled with countless records of achievements at science fairs, math contests, and spelling bees, not to mention her track and field honors. None of the awards seemed to carry much significance for Ellen. Recognition embarrassed her, brought out a sad cynicism that denigrated all honors. Instead of appreciating her accomplishments, her attitude seemed to embody Groucho Marx's line, "Who'd want to belong to a club that would have *me* as a member?"

Carrie and I puzzled over Ellen's plight through breakfast when the phone rang again.

"It's for you," said Carrie with a look of concern.

"Mr. Smith?" asked the nurse. "You're Abraham Smith's son?"

"Yes."

"We admitted your dad through Emergency this morning."

The details were sparse. I knew all I needed to know about hospital admission and was well prepared for Dad's next bout with the "Big C." Each time cancer had reared its ugly head, two other C's had come to Dad's defense – character and chemotherapy. Of the two, I judged the former to be the more potent force. Dad's character, built around a core of optimism and what I judged to be sheer love of life, seemed to wage its own private war against the cancer cells. The glorious landscape that flourished behind his bright eyes had spilled into many a gray moment as I was growing up. Its beauty had retained that power to infiltrate gloom through his – and our – worst hours. Even his battle with cancer had not changed Dad's inner strength and calm. Abe Smith remained, as always, a model of bravery and courage.

The nurse assured me he was well-settled and in no immediate danger. A close friend, who doubled as his landlord, had driven him to the hospital. A best-case scenario would find the two retirees plotting their next fishing trip over the clatter of bedpans and linen carts and the chatter of industrious nurses. The odds dictated otherwise.

My mind was overloaded with the events of recent days and random thoughts that bounced in my brain like mad electrons. My unemployment, my children's futures, encounters with Sophie, and the vivid dreams about a secret Code to Happiness – together they had charged my consciousness with a mix of concern and far-reaching wonder. But the morning phone call from the hospital had brought me back to reality.

My lofty quest would have to wait. Family was the priority for the day. I was off to the hospital.

The Edmund J. Hoppe Hospital is one of our city's architectural treasures – the main building, that is, before they added the boxy new wings, the result of budget-conscious, no-frills efficiency. By the time the Historical Society and local architects and art lovers had formed a coalition to put a hold on the project, the workers had already laid half the pale brick, dashing all hope of matching the look of the original masterpiece.

The long rise of small, cascading steps leading up to the tall front doors made a heavy climb. And even the tall columns loomed like sullen sentries.

The front desk directed me to Dr. Blanchard's office. I wanted to get the straight dope on Dad's condition before I saw him face to face. Dad had his sunny side, but he didn't take well to phony consolation. Repeated bouts with cancer could make a realist of anyone, I speculated.

"Your father keeps battling," said Dr. Blanchard. "But I'm afraid he is losing the war. His cancer has spread."

I could forgive Blanchard his war metaphors. Behind his desk, he had a four-foot wide photograph of the aircraft carrier he had served on before becoming a surgeon.

"Chemotherapy?" I suggested. "Can he go another round?"

"I don't think so. He's had enough. My recommendation is that we just do what we can to control the pain." Blanchard evened a stack of paperwork on his desk. "He's an amazing man, your father," he added.

"You don't have to tell me. How's he doing now?"

"He's hanging in there like a terrier," said Blanchard. "He's asked us to go easy on the pain medication except at night. Says he can't think as clearly as he'd like. He doesn't like being groggy. Says he wants to appreciate everything."

We sat wordless, then rose together. Blanchard walked me to the door.

"They don't make many like him," the doctor said.

I just nodded.

I approached Dad's hospital room with quiet steps. Dad was sitting up in his bed, reading his favorite book, *Moby Dick*, for what I guessed was the fifth or sixth time. The book hung at an obtuse angle between his thumb and forefinger. His head rocked in broken rhythms on a corner of a propped pillow.

"Don't you ever get tired of that book?" I asked

"Hell, it gets better every time," he said. A smile slowly spread across his face.

A half dozen fishing magazines and several resort brochures littered his bed. No matter what his condition, Dad refused to stop thinking about the future, which generally meant another fishing trip.

"How are you, Dad?"

"Great, great," he said. "The rumors of my demise have been greatly exaggerated." He loved that line. "Who said that? Mark Twain? Hemingway?"

"Both of them," I said.

Despite his obviously weakened physical state, I tried to size up his mental condition. "So what's the story?" I asked. "I get the feeling you're planning another walleye trip."

Dad looked up. His eyes flickered with a mischief that belied his condition.

"I got a few tricks left up my sleeve," he said.

I settled into the hard vinyl visitor's chair beside the bed. The hospital made sure you didn't get too comfortable if you weren't paying for a bed.

"Actually, I've been thinking," he went on. "If I get out of here, what do you say we hit the Bay of Quinte? I hear the walleye have been running big in the bay. One last walleye for the wall before I hang up my rods."

I marveled at his outlook. He almost seemed serious. Hanging a fish on the wall was another matter. He hadn't kept a big fish for 10 years or more. He took more pleasure from watching them swim away. He liked to think of fish he had caught and released as still there for his son and grandchildren to catch...or there to swim untouched, in obscurity, to the end of their days.

"I know what you're thinking," Dad went on. "The old man ain't going to make it this time. Navy's probably filled your head with doom and gloom." Navy was his nickname for Dr. Blanchard.

"You have another rebound left in you, I'd wager."

Dad shoved a bookmark in the place his forefinger had held and set the book on the bed stand.

"I'm no fool. I know I'm running out of time," he said without a trace of fear or self-pity. "But I'm going to soak up as much time as I have coming my way and try to wrap up some loose ends..." He smiled. Abe Smith obviously had another goal or two to complete. What they were, I might never know.

I mentioned my conversation with Ellen that morning. She was my dad's dearest joy, and, it seemed, always his biggest concern. I tried to redirect the conversation, but he would have nothing of it. Not even cancer could distract him where his granddaughter's well-being was concerned.

Thirty minutes later, fatigue got the better of him.

Just before he fell asleep, he said, "It's all about *appreciation*."

I watched my dad sleep peacefully and thought about his life. He loved fish and everything about their world. For him, nature was a gallery of art treasures graced with beauty and utilitarian elegance. Whenever he was on the water, he was grateful that these finned creatures had lured him into their world.

As I thought back to our countless fishing trips and the loving details in every one of Dad's rhapsodic lectures about the fish and the art of fishing, the depth of his gratitude for virtually everything that fell into his path in life became apparent. He was a master at getting the most out of life and turning adversity into advantage.

He could turn an old sock into a king's robe.

I recalled Doc Bradshaw's words: "...he wants to *appreciate* what's happening."

What did appreciation mean to a man in a hospital bed when the doctors had no hope?

I watched my father sleep as the afternoon crawled along. His face seemed incongruously serene despite his labored breathing.

Dad had found enchantment in the world and in everything he touched. That cancer could claim him seemed, on one level, contrary to everything I had known him to be – a source of tremendous energy and strength and a shield against adversity.

I waited patiently for him to awake. I wanted another glimpse into my father's soul. What stock had he stored there? What resources remained to serve him in his final hours?

His last words before sleep hung in the silence: "It's all about appreciation."

Appreciation. Perhaps he had been teaching me its lessons throughout his life and I never fully realized it.

How often did we find ourselves complaining about what we don't have instead of enjoying the blessings in our midst? You could waste a lifetime wanting things that would ultimately have little impact on happiness.

"I can lie here in this bed and complain that it's uncomfortable and the food is lousy," he had said. "Or I can appreciate the fact that I'm surrounded by virtual strangers who are caring for me as if I were a member of their family. I can sit here and think about all the fishing trips we might never be able to take, or I can appreciate all the great trips we've had together."

I tried to soak it all in. I wanted to tell Dad about Sophie's words, my strange dream, and ask him what he thought was the secret to happiness.

But he'd probably think I was crazy.

A nurse came in. She checked Dad's vital signs. He woke up and seemed ready to talk again, but the thermometer shut him up.

I witnessed a rare moment of impatience in my father. He caught himself and bit the thermometer. Then he took a deep breath and awaited the nurse's return.

Dad prided himself on his patience. A man who hated stereotypes and labels, he frequently and unabashedly subscribed to one himself. He was a fisherman, and he loved the metaphor as much as the pursuit itself. He latched on to everything noble and virtuous fishing stood for – mostly patience and persistence – and a little dose of guile when he needed it.

Of course, to satisfy his insatiable sense of humor, he was more than willing to draw from the angler's less flattering images as well.

"You know what a fisherman is?" he had asked so many times during my youth that our whole household had learned to shout the answer in unison. "A jerk on one end of the line waiting for a jerk on the other!"

Our groans and baiting had only added to his delight.

The nurse removed the thermometer.

"That wasn't so bad now, was it?" he said, momentarily confusing the aide. Then to me he whispered, "Do they think they can shut me up with that?" His head fell back, and he drew a few quick breaths.

"Where does appreciation fit in with happiness?" I asked when he had settled again into a comfortable breathing rhythm.

"Happiness?" He pondered the question, shifted his weight with clear discomfort. "What does an old walleye fisherman know about happiness? Hell, sometimes you catch 'em. Sometimes you don't. Happiness is how you feel when you catch 'em."

"I'm serious, Dad," I interjected.

"It all starts there," Dad said, with a more serious tone in his voice.

"Where?"

"With appreciation. Happiness starts with appreciation. Without appreciating your skills, your gifts, your opportunities – without appreciating your basic worth as a human being – it's hard to accomplish much of anything." He paused. "It's impossible to enjoy life without appreciation," he said. "Appreciation also opens the door to a smile and then laughter. Appreciation is oxygen for the ember of love, Son. We don't really love anyone until we appreciate who they really are.

"Appreciation makes us aware – not of how big or strong or rich we might be one day, but how big and strong and wealthy we already are," Dad went on. "Appreciation offers possibility. It's that first link to tomorrow's potential. We need to water and nurture it, like a planted seed. But, without that seed, nothing grows."

The speech had robbed him of breath. He took a minute to gather himself.

"I remember you once telling me that what first looks like a problem, a setback, often becomes the best thing that ever happened to us," I said. "You said there are lessons in losses. We just need to appreciate them."

Dad nodded and continued. "Appreciation also opens the door to loving and being loved. It may help us to find the love of others. Appreciation may lead us to a discovery of our own potential. It keeps our head above water, so that we can catch our breath. The more we appreciate what we each have in life, the better we breathe."

And, for a brief moment, it appeared that Dad was breathing better, too.

A young aide in candy stripes took a quick look at Dad's water pitcher and supplies. She poured a fresh glass of water, replaced the old wash cloth with a fresh one. Dad nodded as she mopped his forehead.

A part of me was restless, anxious to press the discussion to completion. Dad smiled. But he was tired again. I could see it in his face.

"Patience, Smith," he said. "You don't need all the answers all at once."

"I know. An angler is nothing without patience," I answered, echoing his lifelong advice.

"You have to let life unfold," he added. "You have to give the good things a chance to flower. But along the way…all along the way…appreciate what you have."

Dad's thoughts settled in, and we sat in silence for a while. For a moment, I thought he had nodded off.

"What about you?" he muttered.

"What?"

"I said, what about you? Everyone is so damned concerned about how I'm doing. What's going on in your life?"

"I lost my job," I said a little sheepishly. An incongruous smile came to Dad's face.

"No big deal." He smiled gently. "It'll probably be the best thing that could have happened to you. Wait and see."

"Thanks for the support, old man!"

His laugh couldn't get past the cough stage.

"I'm glad to bring joy to the infirm," I said when the cough had passed.

"I remember you as a kid with a head full of ideas, almost ready to bust open with enthusiasm." He looked me in the eyes soberly. "I haven't seen that light in your eyes for a long time. Appreciation is more than smelling the flowers or watching the sunset, although that's a piece of it. Appreciate the chance to explore a new path. To do something different."

I struggled with my next thought.

"Do you have any regrets, Dad?" I asked.

"You mean besides bringing another Smith into the world? I mean, how many more of us can the world handle?"

We both chuckled.

"You're a Smith," he reminded me. "That means that, on the surface, you're just an average Joe…from humanity's mainstream…neither royalty nor robber baron." He leaned forward, and I could almost read the deeply etched lines in his face like a road map. His eyes blazed. "That means people have to know you to realize how special you really are. And you have to know yourself. That's a gift to them, and a gift to you."

I studied my dad with quiet admiration.

"Only one," he said.

"Only one what, Dad?"

"Only one regret."

"What's that?"

"That I'll be missing that course in ballroom dancing. Supposed to start next week."

That was Dad. Fitting it all in. That was his biggest challenge.

Until now.

I tried to picture him on the dance floor.

"Ballroom dancing?!!" I asked.

Dad finally slept. I shut off the light and walked downstairs to the cafeteria where I made lunch of a small sandwich, banana, and a carton of milk. By the time I had returned to the room, it looked like evening. Trees were soughing. Raindrops were dancing in the parking lot. Dad's head had sunk deeply into the pillow, and I thought about this remarkable man and the largely uncelebrated life he had lived. I had more questions to ask. But he just slept. After a while, I grabbed the mandatory hospital fare – the cup of red gelatin – from his neglected tray and raised a spoonful in salute. Then, with tears in my eyes, I kissed him on the head and left for home.

The rain pelted me on the way home. I felt like a soaking wet retriever. Puddles formed at my feet.

I called for Carrie when I walked into the house.

A note on the refrigerator reminded me that she had a meeting at the library that evening.

I took off my wet shoes and clothing, dried my hair with a towel, donned a robe and moved to the study. I'd wait up for Carrie, but in the meantime, I had something to do. My mind raced with thoughts that I didn't want to lose.

An empty notebook lay on the corner of my desk. I grabbed a pen from the desk drawer, penned *The Socrates Smith Notebook* in my best script on the cover, opened the notebook, and began to write.

The Socrates Smith Notebook

Conversation with Dad:
A lesson in appreciation.

Dad's life has been a lesson in appreciating everything thrown his way. Why should his final days be any different?

What do I appreciate? What should I appreciate more than I do?

"I don't want to get to the end of my life and find that I have just lived the length of it. I want to have lived the width of it as well."
   -Diane Ackerman

"It is no use to grumble and complain;
It's just as cheap and easy to rejoice;
When God sorts out the weather and sends
rain - Why, rain's my choice."
   -James Whitcomb Riley

"There is no such thing as bad weather, only different kinds of good weather."
     -John Ruskin

"Blessings we enjoy daily; and for most of them, because they are so common, most men forget to pay their praise."
     -Izaak Walton

"Reflect upon your present blessings, of which every man has plenty; not on your past misfortunes of which all men have some."
     -Charles Dickens

"The universe is change; our life is what our thoughts make of it."
     -Marcus Aurelius Antoninus

"Life consists not in holding good cards but in playing those you hold well."
  -Josh Billings

"People travel to wonder at the height of the mountains, at the huge waves of the seas, at the long course of the rivers, at the vast compass of the ocean, at the circular motion of the stars, and yet they pass by themselves without wondering."
  -Saint Augustine

"Millions long for immortality who do not know what to do with themselves on a rainy Sunday afternoon."
  -Susan Ertz

"The invariable mark of wisdom is to see the miraculous in the common."
  -Ralph Waldo Emerson

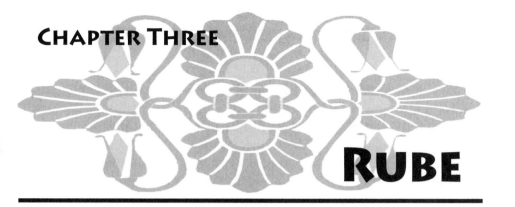

CHAPTER THREE

RUBE

The DΣLPHI was alive with a fresh cast of characters the following morning. I sat down at the counter in front of Sophie, but she pointed to an empty table near the back wall and asked me to move there. The sports page lay open on the table behind me. It was that glorious time of the year where the spectator sports converged. Baseball had entered its post-season. Football was in full swing. Hockey, too, had opened, and basketball teams had begun their pre-season games.

The wall beside me was filled with photos of celebrities. If there was anything George Niketopoulous took more pride in than his coffee, it was the photographs that hung on his walls like loose-fitting tiles. I often entertained myself at the DΣLPHI by identifying the movie stars, news anchors, politicians, and, more than anything else, sports stars George shamelessly passed off as friends and patrons. George swore that he had met everyone featured on his walls. I assumed that excluded the handful of men and women shown in the sepia-toned shots. Still, I liked those shots best. They gave the wall a gallery-like quality.

A remarkable photograph hung at eye-level beside my table. A baseball player turning a double play was suspended above the cloud of dust and flying spikes of a menacing base runner. The photo reflected a bygone era with flat-crowned caps and uniforms plumped with air. It was one of my favorites. The second baseman was poised high, right arm extended at the point of release, legs yielding to slashing spikes.

"Do you recognize him?"

A distinguished gentleman with silver hair and dancing eyes smiled at me from the neighboring table. He was dressed in a sport shirt, handsomely draped by a blue blazer. An open book lay face down on the table.

"Can't say I do," I said.

"Yes. Some say he was quite a player in his time," he said.

"And when was his time?"

"Before yours!" he laughed. "His name's Harold Robertson. They called him Rube."

"It's a great photo," I said. "I wonder how George came up with it."

"I gave it to him," he said, extending his hand. "Hi, I'm Rube Robertson."

"Pleased to meet you," I said, enjoying the surprise.

I liked Robertson immediately. His silver gray hair rose above his brow in a frozen wave ready to break. Curling around his ears, it gave him a look of wild energy that contrasted interestingly with his otherwise neat look of sophistication. His face was sun-darkened and slightly blotched from the accumulation of too much sun – his solitary loss to Father Time.

He wore a gold band on his left hand, the hand that beckoned me to join him at his table.

"So, how do you get Rube from Harold?" I asked, settling across from him.

"It's a nickname from the early days in the majors. Rube, as in 'bumpkin,'" he smiled. "You know, that's how they tried to keep us strong country boys in their place back when I entered the bigs…Make them feel out of their element in the big city. I was 19 years old, and the only flush toilet I had used was in the train station on my way to meet the team. My coaches and teammates noticed how I was fascinated with just about everything in the city, from the libraries to the Tiffany lampshades in the hotel lobbies to the steps at City Hall. 'Look at this rube, will ya?' said Buck Wilson, the center fielder. He saw me looking wide-eyed before those two bronze sculptures of Indians on horses in Chicago on the way to play the White Sox. The name stuck."

He recounted his baseball career, which seemed fascinating and, at times, hilarious. He sprinkled anecdotes of locker room pranks with casual references to sports icons like Gehrig, Ruth, and a young kid named DiMaggio, whom he played against in his final season.

He could still spin a tale like a lot of good ol' country boys, with dry wit, well-chosen detail, and neat twists that caught you unaware.

But many, many decades had passed since anyone had mistaken "Rube" Robertson for a bumpkin, no matter how self-effacing he was during those cherished years in the major leagues.

But his dance on baseball's big stage was all too short. He was a passionate, fearless player, and his career ended abruptly. He'd had five home runs in eight games and a 14-game hitting streak when he attempted to break up a double play with a barreling move at second base. The consequences smashed whatever brash sense of invulnerability he had carried with him his first 23 years. His spike caught the ground as he began to roll, tearing knee ligaments and registering a lightning bolt of pain in his brain. His shoulder caught the opposing shortstop's leaping knee. The impact severed his clavicle and tore shoulder tissue. His career was over.

I had often wondered about people, particularly prominent sports figures, whose lives had peaked early and who drifted – or plummeted – from the highest summit into obscurity. How did they fare in life after a brief taste of glory? Did they take their thirst for success into other realms with less glamour but fair reward? Or did they curse their fate, turn bitter, and squander their gifts and opportunities? Sensing that these subjects wouldn't bother an old war-horse like Rube, I found myself asking him these very questions.

"I confess: I brooded," he said. "For a little while, at least. I was in the prime of my life. I had felt indestructible."

Rube took a long sip from his mug and pushed it aside. He went on.

"All I could sense was the sickening quiet of my life. My career in baseball was over in an instant. They didn't have sophisticated surgical techniques for the knees back then. I tried to make a comeback, but it wasn't meant to be. It wasn't long before I had left baseball, and I had nothing else to do but rest, day in and day out. Rest and think."

"What did you think about?"

"Well, at first, I dwelled on the injuries. That was a dead, bitter end. After a short while, I changed my focus. I decided I'd do something useful. I wasn't sure what, but I began to look at life with a new pair of eyes. Trying to look for opportunities, not problems.

"One day, I even found myself back at the ballpark, watching my old teammates practice. I remember looking at the gloves that were lying in the corner of the dugout. The gloves were well broken in, if you know what I mean. Torn laces, brown leather turned black with oil and age and ball diamond dust.

"'What are you doing with these, Hank?' I asked the equipment manager. 'Giving 'em away…throwing 'em out. Hell, I don't know!' he says. So I say, 'Why don't you give a couple to a washed up infielder?' 'Suit yourself,' Hank says, and he drops the bunch of them into a canvas bag and tosses it to me. He even throws in a pair of spikes with the soles starting to separate from the leather.

"Well, I look at those baseball gloves that night, and I see that they're designed all wrong. They damn near map the hand, like a kid's stencil of his fingers. The webbing is weak, too. All these years, and how many thousands – maybe millions – of baseball gloves had been worn? Hadn't anyone seen the opportunity to build a better mitt? The glove was an extension of the hand, not just a covering. Let it do what the hand could not. Make the pocket deeper. Let it close around the ball. Give it better reach. Make the fingers longer. Some other things, too, but you get the idea.

"I call the glove manufacturer the next day. He listens to what I have to say. Much to my surprise, he tells me he'll be passing through town the next week, so we schedule a meeting. By this time, I've drawn pictures of my new glove. I'm afraid he's going to think they look like something out of science fiction. Well, turns out, he's blown away! Only thing, though, he was concerned about the old guardian angels – the protectors of baseball purity, you know – who might reject them simply because they are new and different. He's afraid they'll be hard to sell to the big league teams.

"'Let me do it,' I say. 'I'll sell them!' And guess what? Sell them I did! Heck, he liked my design so much, he gave me a job in his sales department, and I became his number one salesman for the next thirty or so years."

I paused to absorb the quality of man that I was sharing coffee with. His integrity and honesty was so obvious that I could see where he'd be a natural salesman. "So you got a job designing and selling baseball gloves?"

"No, I *had fun* designing and selling baseball gloves. I found a good business opportunity, too. But most importantly, I found the value of curiosity."

"Curiosity?" I asked. Now *I* was curious.

"Wonderment. The thing that keeps you young," said Rube. "By the way, what are you doing today?"

"No particular plans. Why?"

"We could use a golf partner. One of our foursome dropped out."

"I'm not much of a golfer," I warned.

"It will give us a chance to talk…we're not that good either, but it's a lot of fun."

"I'll get my clubs."

A coffee urn intruded on our space.

"I see you handsome gentlemen have met," said Sophie, winking at me.

"He was admiring my photograph," said Rube. "You can never have too many fans."

"Just like you can never have enough big tippers," said Sophie, tapping Rube thankfully on the shoulder. She spun around behind him and pointed at my new acquaintance, nodding her assent. "Maybe you can learn something from this guy, Socrates Smith."

"Socrates?" Rube repeated as Sophie sped away.

"It's just a nickname," I blushed. "Just call me Smith."

Second thoughts nagged me as I headed to Youngfield Country Club. My bag was freshly free of the cobwebs that had grown over the club heads since last spring. I was worried about how I'd play with three regular golfers.

Rube approached me with a conspicuous limp as I pulled into the country club. For a moment, I wondered if he wasn't a bit older than he appeared.

"Socrates Smith…meet General Howard," said Rube.

The general had that lean, hard look of a lifelong Marine, ever ready to answer a country's crisis…or enter a barroom brawl. His face was leathery, with a simple road map of expressive wrinkles etched by weather and duty in his forehead and cheeks as well as at the corners of his eyes.

"Socrates?" he repeated.

"Just call me Smith."

The other man, a clean-cut gentleman who looked to be in his 50s, introduced himself as Jason Gardner. On a hunch, I asked if he was the same Gardner who owned Gardner Boats and Marine Supplies not far from my home.

"The very same," he said.

I had hoped to pick up my conversation with Rube. He had seemed on the verge of some revelation. Sophie's gesture had me convinced it had something to do with the Code. But these gentlemen had other things on their mind – golf, and golf, but mostly golf.

We loaded our clubs on the golf cart. I was paired with Rube. Seeing the group's intensity, I forced my attention to the game at hand. I loosened up with some rusty swings and an assortment of stretches.

"Our usual wager?" asked the general.

"Absolutely," answered Rube. The general and Gardner cast quizzical glances at me. "Count Smith in, too," he said, walking to the first tee and whispering "I've got you covered." He stopped and winked. "You better be good!"

Rube made good company. As serious and businesslike as he was on the tees and greens, he conversed freely as we cruised along the course. He drove our golf cart as if we were on Mr. Toad's Wild Ride, and I held onto the roof just to keep myself within the cart's confines. Whenever I was able to catch my breath, we talked and learned a little bit about each other along the way.

"Not bad for a 90-year-old?" Rube stated out loud after sinking a long putt.

"Ninety?!!!" I exclaimed. "You've got to be kidding!"

"He had a birthday last week," confirmed the general

I learned a fair amount about Rube over the next few holes, and I found myself amazed at each revelation.

Robertson was a hybrid jack-of-all-trades/renaissance man – country-style, of course. His life appeared to be an odd assortment of hobbies, passions, business success, and social service. The range of Robertson's interests, it seemed, was endless.

The design and sale of baseball gloves was just the beginning. The crusade for better baseball equipment took him to big cities, tiny burgs, and just about every town that had ever heard of baseball in between. I could imagine how he pitched his vision of the game to his customers, mixing the national pastime and its hallowed traditions with the excitement of a new generation of ballplayers breaking through old barriers. He spoke of pitchers hurling the stitched sphere 100 miles per hour, of home run hitters with unprecedented power, of daring base runners breaking Ty Cobb's stolen base mark.

He visited a lot of sporting goods stores, too, and began to study the equipment on the shelves and on floor displays. He helped design and then sell training devices for pitchers and gizmos to improve hitting.

Remembering his injury and the leather brace he had created, he sought out manufacturers and research clinics to come up with new designs for protective gear, braces, helmets, and pads for all the major sports.

During his travels, he visited museums and art galleries. He read books on all sorts of topics. Mysteries were his first love, but he also loved Mark Twain. Later in his life, Rube developed a love for backpacking into wilderness areas. He seemed to have immersed himself in a variety of new activities over the years, taking a childlike delight in each new experience.

His sparkling eyes told the story. Rube Robertson tried to make a new world each day. Even at 90, he was just a happy, curious kid.

The rust on my golf game was conspicuous from the first tee. I had sliced my opening drive into the rough, then watched in amazement as the rest of my foursome drilled their drives down the middle of the fairway.

The general carried the big stick, walloping the golf ball with sharp, audible authority. His drives came low off the tee. They seemed to rocket at eyeball level until they had traveled a hundred yards or so. Gardner was a tactician, considering clubs and conditions carefully, positioning his next shot like a pool hall hustler on a 50-ball run.

But it was Rube who was the most impressive. He filled me in on the layout of the course, the quickness of the greens, the treachery of bunkers and sand traps, and the position of the pin. I had never met anyone so taken with the details of the game. Yet he did it in a most relaxed, matter-of-fact manner, without the teeth-gritting intensity that sucked the life out of the game for a casual player like me.

Rube's stroke became more fluid and graceful with each hole. Watching him reminded me of a story I had once heard about Arturo Toscanini, the famous conductor of the New York Symphony Orchestra and the NBC Orchestra. Late in his career and well into his 80s, he was enfeebled with arthritis. So slow and weak had his movements become that he had to be assisted to the conductor's dais by two aides. At first, he waved the conductor's baton modestly with short and measured strokes. But as the symphony rose and the music resonated through the auditorium, the man became transformed. Soon his arms were cutting full, energetic arcs through the air, evoking, in turn, even more life and fullness from each instrument. The legend of Toscanini was born from this magic mix of love and enthusiasm. It was a similar enthusiasm and love of life that I admired now in Rube.

I basked in the beauty of the day, urging on my new friend, and along the way returning some modest respectability to my own golf game. I saved the seventeenth hole for Rube and me with a fine chip shot. But it was Rube who bailed us out on the final hole with a long putt. Gardner groaned. General Howard stood impassive and reached into the jacket draped over the back of his cart.

"Who's the check to today?" asked the general.

"To Edmund J. Hoppe Hospital," said Rube. He turned to me and added: "My charity of choice."

The General and Gardner headed off to their appointments. Rube and I retired to the clubhouse for a cold drink.

He spoke briefly about our round of golf, but we were soon on to other topics. I learned that he was a trustee of the local art gallery and helped sponsor several new artists. I gathered that his encouragement had worked wonders on their confidence. Now their work was starting to take off.

"Tell me what you know about the Code," I asked after the waiter had taken our order.

"What code is that?" Robertson asked innocently.

"Sophie told me I could learn something from you," I replied. "I thought perhaps you might know something about this secret Code to Happiness."

"So this is where the Socrates part comes in," Rube smiled. He dabbed at the corner of his mouth with the napkin. The back of his hand was mottled with liver spots.

"'Smith' will do."

"I'm no philosopher, though I've read a little…and plan to read more," he said.

"But you do seem to be a happy man."

"Well, I can't remember ever wanting to trade places with anyone, so I guess I am."

"Not even after the collision at second base?"

"That could be the one exception," he said and fell silent. "But the self-pity didn't last long."

"It sounded like you were off to a great career, maybe a trip to Cooperstown."

"I overstated my worth. I was young, just getting going. Still had a lot to prove."

"No, seriously," I insisted. "The world is full of angry, disappointed people who think life dealt them a bad hand. They go on saying year after year, 'If only this or that.' You were doing something you loved and had a shot at greatness."

"And I lost everything and somehow came out ahead," he said. His eyes were bright and challenging and bore no trace of regret.

He went on, "True, I lay in that hospital bed for days. I caught a glimpse of what my future *could* have been. Baseball was the bright star that had led me out of my small town. But it wasn't the last stop on my train ride. Hell, in retrospect, it wasn't even the most interesting. Look at all the things I have done, at all the people I have met!"

Rube took a sip from the glass of Australian wine he had ordered on the waiter's recommendation. He nodded his approval and went on.

"If you want to keep life fresh and exciting, there's nothing more important than a fresh pair of eyes and a spirit that wants to see more, do more, and learn more."

"I see what you mean. I never would have guessed you were ninety years old."

Rube chuckled and nodded at the compliment. There was a lull while he gathered his thoughts, and, for a brief moment, I could see that age had not passed him by; he had simply learned to travel with it gracefully.

"Youthful curiosity, I call it," Rube said finally. "That's what keeps life new and interesting. That's what makes a person look forward to each day. It keeps you from falling into the rut of old habits, of old ways of thinking. Unfortunately, too many people are afraid of trying something new. 'New' forces you to adjust, to adapt! Too many people are afraid of change. And that kind of fear just plain cuts off life. Can I do things differently? Will I succeed? Does this new way of looking at something mean that I was wrong the first time? These thoughts can scare people, make them retreat when they could be enjoying their new possibilities."

"By that standard, a lot of young people are old before their time," I suggested.

"That's the problem! The other day I met a man in his late 40s. He had been laid off from his job as an auto body repairman. He had hated the job, and the dust had him coughing all the time.

"But even with a fair severance, he was despondent. 'I don't want to go back to the body shop,' he complained. 'But I can't do anything else.' *Can't do anything else!* Do you believe it? A man not yet 50 years old who says he can't do anything else? He's giving up. Instead of using the time he has been given to explore new possibilities, he had chosen to give up. He's resigned himself to a life he hates. Why not see what the world has to offer? Open a new door! Hell, I remember waking up on my sixty-fifth birthday and thinking 'I wonder what I'll be doing when I get old?'"

"What *are* you going to do?" I deadpanned.

"Maybe join the Marines and see the world."

We both smiled.

"You know, a man with avid curiosity and passionate interests has no limits," Rube declared. His eyes burned into me as he made his point. "Think of some of your old schoolmates, the ones whom the teachers regarded as slow learners and probably gave up on early. I'll bet at least one of those guys learned just about everything there is to know about something: cars, construction, golf. Doesn't really matter what."

"David Krantz," I said.

"Who's that?"

"He's the guy you're talking about from my school days," I said. "We didn't think he could spell his own name, but when we got into high school and beyond, we'd take our car problems to him. It didn't seem that there was anything about automobiles he either didn't know or couldn't figure out."

"We all know people like that," smiled Rube. "A lot of them became very successful. When they finally find out what turns them on, their enthusiasm takes over. Their capacity to learn anything and everything about the subject seems limitless. Just as important, that passion seems contagious. Other people trust and believe in them. They just get a good feeling: 'This guy knows what he's doing!'"

Rube sipped the last drops of wine in his glass, leaned on his elbows, and craned his neck toward me.

"Take that kind of curiosity into your world each day…There's no limit to the joy it will bring your life."

The city had grown peaceful and shadowy but for the thin spread of traffic and the city lights. I called Carrie and told her I'd be home in a little while. I decided to circle back into the downtown area. A light was on at the DΣLPHI, and a couple of workers attended to after hours clean-up. I waited for several minutes, hoping to find Sophie, though, as far as I knew, she seldom worked the evenings.

The last customer pushed through the door, and one of the attendants locked the door behind him.

I turned the ignition, looked back at the DΣLPHI and paused.

In the window was a tall, thin glass vase with a single red rose. Beyond it, and clearly visible on the sidewalk, was an old Pepsi billboard with a slogan I had seen many times but had never really noticed. Next to a Pepsi bottle was a picture of a man and the simple slogan, "For those who think young!" The man might have passed for a young version of Rube Robertson.

The Socrates Smith Notebook

Conversation with Rube Robertson:
A lesson in youthful curiosity.

Age is a number. Youthful curiosity is an attitude. What an education one receives observing Rube Robertson. The delight he takes in his relentless pursuits and bottomless barrel of interests is a joy to behold. Ninety years young!

Are men and women born with such freshness and vitality? Why can't these be cultivated traits? I don't think we need to be really young or really old to have a sense of youthful curiosity. Can't we find that same spirit - that same attitude - at any age???

Can we become young as we grow old and wise? What was that quotation??? We must become like little children in order to enter the kingdom of heaven...

Lifelong learning. A willingness to see ideas, beliefs, and the world itself from fresh angles rejuvenates him, keeps him young in spirit. His body seems to respond in kind.

"Who does not grow, declines."
　　　- Rabbi Hillel

"May you have a strong foundation when the winds of change shift...and may you be forever young."
　　　- Bob Dylan

"You are never too old to be what you might have been."
　　　- George Eliot

"I promise to keep on living as though I expect to live forever. Nobody grows old by merely living a number of years. People grow old by deserting their ideals. Years may wrinkle the skin, but to give up wrinkles the soul."
　　　- Douglas MacArthur

"Grow old with me! The best is yet to be."
　　　- Robert Browning

"If you enjoy living, it is not difficult to keep the sense of wonder."
　　　- Ray Bradbury

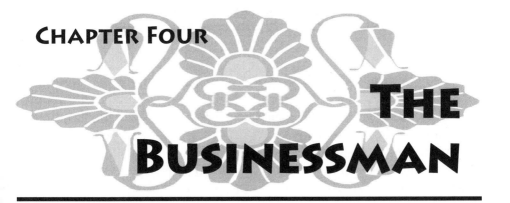

CHAPTER FOUR

THE BUSINESSMAN

Is a dream a window into the unconscious mind, or is it a glimpse of the yet-to-come? Were the otherworldly visions that seemed to guide and direct me now true in a way the senses could not validate? Were these nightly incursions on my consciousness coming from those who lived beyond? Or were my dreams only figments of my all too anxious yearnings?

Such questions begged for attention each morning, and filled the cracks between the remarkable encounters of recent days. Had you asked me weeks earlier about the contents of my last dream, I would have drawn a blank. Now my nights were alive with fantasies, my dreams as vivid as waking life. Characters stepped in and out of my dreams to guide my quest.

Last night, I found myself thigh-high in vapor, shuffling in that slow, effortless gait of a twilight being. An invisible path lay beneath the mist, and I followed its road markers. Occasionally, the guideposts proved to be people who pointed this way and that and gestured toward the road ahead.

One of the guides was Rube Robertson; he appeared twisted and craggy, like an oak tree, from afar, but who became youthful and bright-eyed as I neared him. He pointed ahead, and we briefly fell in step together, his arm crooked around my shoulders. He patted my back and fed me encouragement with words I could not decipher…until the sounds of the Smith household returned me to that other life I knew.

Carrie's clatter in the kitchen cut through Randy's excited ramblings. Eddie whooped with excitement.

"What's going on, guys?" I asked

"Geez, Dad. Put on some real pants, will you?" urged Eddie. He obviously didn't care for the long-lost bright green pants I was wearing that were popular about fifteen years ago. I had found them in the attic a few days earlier while looking for something else and had decided to put them on to wear while I did some yard work.

That's my fifteen-year old. Everything I did embarrassed him.

"Please do," added Carrie, trying hard not to smile.

"What's the matter?" I asked, feigning ignorance.

"Gross, Dad," said Eddie. I looked again at Carrie.

"Those pants are hideous," she agreed, now in full smile.

"What's all the chatter about?" I asked, conceding defeat and trying to change the subject.

"Randy's gonna be famous!" declared Eddie.

"Oh, yeah? What happened?"

"I got this gig over at The Burrow," said Randy. "We started last night...You wouldn't believe how things are coming together."

"The crowd liked you?"

"The place was rocking," interjected Eddie before Randy had a chance to answer.

"Interesting. And how would 15-year-old Eddie Smith happen to know the goings-on at The Burrow?"

Eddie blushed and, suddenly quiet, muttered. "I don't know. I just know what Randy tells me."

I gave Eddie a cold nod, meaning we'd talk later. In a dark club, Eddie could easily pass for 18 or older.

"So. How did it go, Randy?" I asked.

"Randy's going to be the next Barry Manilow," said Carrie, as she snuck up behind him and tickled his ribs. Randy didn't find her joke funny.

"The band has been working on a bunch of new songs that we played last night. It was great!"

He sang a few bars from one song, occasionally inserting drumbeats on the table with his index fingers. I tried to look impressed. Randy broke into a neat falsetto that had Eddie laughing hysterically. My boys were enjoying the moment.

I sought to muster some enthusiasm. It wasn't easy. I had other ideas for my son's future, outside the world of rock and roll. "Sounds great, Randy," I said.

Suddenly, Randy became serious. "They want me to record an album, Dad."

"Yeah?"

"Honest. Can you believe it!?"

"Who's 'they'?"

"Some guys with a recording studio," he said guardedly.

"What studio is that?"

"Blue Records," he said. "It's a new label in town. Pretty cool, huh?"

"That's promising, Randy. Let's talk about it later." I was sorry I couldn't muster more enthusiasm. I was apprehensive, and I'm sure it showed.

Randy stared at the table uneasily, then rose suddenly. "Gotta go," he said, turning and heading out the door before I knew what happened.

"What did I say?" I asked Carrie.

"Geez, Dad," said Eddie. "He thought you'd be happy for him."

Before I could say another word, Eddie ran out to join Randy in sympathetic support.

I puzzled over Randy's response. But I knew he sensed my reservation. Could Randy carve out a place for himself in this giddy world of music? I had no idea. He had talent. He had drive. He had passion. The problem was that Randy's style of music brought him into contact with an element that I distrusted. Behind the stage lights and the heavy metal lurked a dark backdrop of booze, drugs, and other hollow answers to ambitious dreams. And right now, he was single-minded.

Did someone say raising children is easy?

"Socrates Smith. Meet Phillip Stover," said Sophie. That name again. To my surprise, Stover made no comment. Sophie had met me at the door, hooking Stover's arm and halting him in his march out the door like a drifting boat drawn suddenly taut against its anchor cord.

"Pleased to meet you, Smith," he said. I lost my fingers in his meaty paw as we shook hands. I had seen pictures of Stover before in the paper and had watched him duck in and out of the DΣLPHI on occasion, but, standing next to him, he appeared much larger and younger than I had guessed. He wore a big smile.

"You two should spend some time together," said Sophie.

"Is that so?" said the businessman, looking me over curiously as DΣLPHI patrons snaked around us. "If Sophie says so, who am I to argue?" he added, handing me a business card. "Why don't you meet me at my office tomorrow morning? I'll make sure we have time to chat. How's ten o'clock?"

"Perfect," I said, again marveling at how Fate seemed to shape my days. Perhaps, I thought to myself, there might be a job opportunity waiting for me.

"Thank you, Sophie," I said, thinking about that possibility.

I headed to the Schuman Theater. We had tickets to see *The Man of La Mancha*, one of our favorite plays. As I waited for Carrie to arrive, I replayed the events of the day. I had spoken with several friends about job prospects. Each had seemed interesting: a research director, a market analyst, and a director of marketing. As I considered the descriptions from my friends, however, none of the opportunities seemed exciting. I didn't want to settle for just another job if I didn't have to. I recalled Rube's observation about the guy who had drawn a tight box around his capabilities, and I hoped to sidestep jobs that would quickly turn into dull routine. I had a good reputation in the business community, and I was ready to see where that might lead. I knew I had my family to support, but I was optimistic that something interesting would turn up.

Carrie was late. The crowd became more restless as the opening curtain neared. I climbed the base of a statue and clung to the muscled arm of an icon reminiscent of ancient Greek statuary. I scanned the crowd for Carrie.

"How's the view from up there?" The voice came from directly below. Carrie wore a dress of white and peach gossamer. She looked beautiful. I hopped down, told her I loved her, and then gave her a kiss.

We moved cattle-like among the well-dressed crowd, and finally settled in our seats. Minutes later, the orchestra exploded with the overture, an orchestral medley of romantic themes. The curtain rose, unveiling a magnificent set design that drew a gasp from the crowd. The actors' voices rang rich and resonant. Soon, I was engrossed in the play, all my worries and plans lost in the moment.

The highlight of the play, of course, was "The Impossible Dream," Quixote's defining aria. The actor's voice was inspiring in its rich resonance. It surrounded us in the lower registers and reverberated from the upper reaches of the auditorium in the final verse, which ended dramatically with the lyrics "to reach the impossible star."

A chill rushed up my spine and radiated through my limbs. At that moment, I could only think of Randy and his own musical dream. How different was the music, to be sure! No way to compare the biting, strident sounds of Randy's electric guitar with the melodic romance of *The Man of La Mancha*. Still, there I was, making the comparison all the same, pondering Randy as he tilted at his own windmills toward a career in music. It was a career fraught with risks I could only guess at, but it was hard not to admire his passion and ambition.

There was no such thing as an "impossible dream" in Phillip Stover's world. He was a man of dreams, to be sure. But what made him stand out from most earthbound stargazers was his rare talent for transforming hope and visions into reality.

I had soaked up some of his world while waiting in his office that morning. His secretary, Josephine, had escorted me to an elegant chamber that seemed to have been carved out of mahogany rather than built from it. Josephine made sure I was comfortable.

I admired Stover's bookshelves, photos, and collected artifacts. Several business books sat on one shelf. Biographies of famous people filled the rest. It appeared that Stover remained an active learner in spite of his far-reaching business success.

The artifacts intrigued me most. I noticed a strange bowl with a finish that seemed to be of dusty, unevenly textured enamel.

"It's a Buddhist beggar's bowl," said Stover, who smiled in the doorway. "It's made from a human skull." We shook hands. "Not exactly what you expected to find in a businessman's office? I picked it up in Malaysia. It's not at all offensive in that culture."

He settled behind his desk and continued. "I've spent plenty of time in Southeast Asia."

"Business?" I asked.

"Some. A lot of my travel was out of curiosity and personal interest. The Orient is a remarkable place. It's too bad more Westerners don't travel there or, better yet, live there for a while. They don't know what they are missing. They have no idea what it has to offer."

"And what is that?" I asked.

He shrugged. "Perspective. Wonder. Mystery. Different ways of looking at the world that fill you with insight. Yes, you'll find plenty of business opportunities there, too. But opportunities are everywhere. And I find myself far more relaxed and thoughtful when I am in Asia. Business often takes a back seat."

"Interesting," I said.

And interesting he was. Stover enjoyed an eclectic mix of hobbies, studies, and business and cultural pursuits.

He was a collector of art and artifacts and had an encyclopedic grasp of many subjects. At first, I fancied him one of those guys with nightclub memories, able to pull off surprising feats of recall. But as our conversation continued, I understood the remarkable depth of his understanding. He grasped subjects from the inside out. With amazing acumen, he cut to the heart and soul of a matter. Nothing, it seemed, entered Phillip Stover's mind without illuminating some part of the human experience.

At one brief lull in the conversation, I voiced my thanks for the generous gift of his time.

He waved his hand, dismissing my concern as unnecessary. "Sophie indicated this quest is rather important to you."

"Oh…she mentioned that to you? It sounds crazy, but I'm intrigued that there actually may be a secret Code to Happiness."

He nodded knowingly. "I understand," he said without further elaboration.

"Life's lessons," he began again, "unfold in strange ways." His eyes smiled. "The sign posts are everywhere. Mentors and guardians are there at our disposal, ready to lead each of us to our destiny or our goal, lead us to fulfillment. Yet most of us are unwilling to follow that call. Most don't have the faith or can't conjure the guts to follow the course. Some things take time. Others come quickly." He leaned forward and lifted the beggar's bowl. "Knowing or recognizing what's important to you is the first step."

"I'm kinda struggling with that now. I have a lot of responsibilities. A sick father. My family. I've recently been downsized out of a job. I wonder if I'm wasting my time on this hunt for a secret code. I've read enough self-help books that haven't helped much at all." I paused briefly before continuing. "I've found myself wondering whether the hunt to unlock the secret Code to Happiness is just another indulgence. Maybe I should spend my time on other – more important – things."

"You're not the first seeker nagged with doubt," Stover said, and I sensed that he understood my concern all too well. "On the other hand, if there is a Code to Happiness, maybe it will help you deal better with your important day to day responsibilities.

"You'll have to make your own decisions and trust your instincts on which path to follow," he went on. "Sometimes you don't know if you have wings until you take the leap."

There was something I needed to ask Stover. "I understand what you are saying," I began. "But – and believe me, I mean no disrespect – isn't it much easier to talk about risk and to take risks when you're backed by wealth, staffs of people, and all sorts of assets? Then, you can think, a mistake? A loss here or there? No big deal. I mean your position gives you a chance to focus on happiness. Maybe that's a luxury most people can't afford."

To my sweet relief, my challenge did not faze Phillip Stover in the slightest. He nodded, whether in agreement or in simple understanding of my thoughts, I was not sure.

"Let me tell you a story," he said.

"In the middle of empty."

That's how Phillip Stover described his childhood home on a small farm in the Midwest. The farmland was rich and capable of growing nearly anything a person could need or want. That the people around him were so destitute strikes him as puzzling and ironic to this day.

Of course, it was "rural poor," he explained. "It's not quite the same as the poverty that comes with urban blight. With a decent plot of land, you could grow a lot of your own food. Hunger was not an enormous problem in most years, though there were a few winters and springs when meat came in very short supply and another couple of summers when drought or insects took their toll on the crops. But we were ramshackle poor just the same."

Stover was a middle child in a 10-kid family. His father had emigrated from what had been Austria-Hungary at the time. "Forever" was the outlook for the unchanging lives of the local families – forever in need, forever harsh, a forever chain of hopeless days.

That was the backdrop for the childhood of Phillip Stovec. (A clerical error would change his name to "Stover," and the young man would regard the mistake as part of his ticket out of a world that his brothers had perceived as beyond escape.)

Often, he would gaze out over the ridges of farm land and imagine an ocean there, an ocean that would take him to exotic lands he had read about in the novels and travel books that teachers shared with him almost conspiratorially. His family found his pleasure in reading odd, a sign of a poor work ethic and questionable character.

He had other dreams, too. More practical ones. They were dreams that lifted him above the tedium of the town that had grown up around the farm. He would occasionally hike to the farms to the south and west to look at the homes of the more successful farmers, homes that were sided with white-painted pine and boasted thick columns on the front porch. They looked like Southern plantations to young Phillip. He guessed their interiors were more handsome and luxurious than any he had seen. He imagined the rooms filled with tall hardwood bookshelves, their thick tomes in proper order. When he found these farmhouses held much plainer rooms later, his visions remained undamaged. There had to be places like those he envisioned somewhere, and he would find them one day.

Ironically, his break came during a hostile encounter that would rupture the Stovec household. Stanley, the oldest son still living at home, discovered a book that Phillip had hidden beneath the old mattress that served as a bed for both Phillip and his younger brother, Steven. Strong and bull-like, Stanley worked on the farm and shouldered the burdens of grown men. He had little tolerance for the pursuits of "men with soft hands," as he called them. He taunted Phillip about the book until the insults turned into blows. With a violent shove, Stanley pinned Phillip against the wall. Stanley's thick, work-hardened body pressed against Phillip, rendering him immobile. An odor of sweat and rage overwhelmed him.

To make a mocking example of what he thought his younger brother had become, Stanley released his grip momentarily to grab one of the scarves his mother wore as a babushka. Phillip slipped loose from the relaxed grip, lunged for the shovel the family used to add coal to the iron-bellied stove, and whacked Stanley across the knees with all the strength he could muster.

The fleeing Phillip, not yet 16 years old, flew out the door amid the roar and stream of his brother's invectives and the feeling that he would likely never see house nor family again. Still, in his hurry, he had the presence of mind to grab the book that had precipitated the incident.

He didn't look back.

In the black of early morning, Phillip hopped aboard an empty freight car headed east.

His next days were nightmarish. He dodged the railroad men, hid in tall weeds near the tracks, nervously ate a bowl of stew he begged for in a hobo town. He boarded the next train that passed the camp when fear of spending the night among so many gritty men with puzzling eyes took hold.

He did not leave the safety of the rails until he hit a small bustling town in Pennsylvania.

He liked the water tower and the peaceful sounds of the birds when the train halted for freight exchange. At the moment he heard the birds, he looked out at the rounded mountains. He fell in love with the trees, the likes of which he had never seen before.

He settled into the town for a short while, securing a job in a grocery store and the use of a small supply room for sleeping quarters. When he had earned enough money and learned to sew well enough that he could hide his money in the thick seams of his pant legs, he went back to the train station and listened again to the birds that had signaled him there. Then he hopped aboard the early morning train headed to Baltimore.

◇◇◇◇

"Money factored little into my thoughts at the time," Stover explained. "I clung to hope. Hope...and my dreams. When fear was about to get the best of me, my dreams gave me courage. When I felt lost and aimless, my dreams pointed toward a destination.

In his dreams, there had always been an ocean.

"My first hint of big water was a view of Chesapeake Bay near Baltimore. The harbor held a mix of freighters along with a few tall ships with furled canvas that seemed to have entered the 20th century through a time warp. The docks bustled with activity. I tried to imagine where the barrels stacked on sturdy pallets would end up."

He ate a crab cake in a small restaurant filled with dockworkers and decided he had never tasted anything so good.

He needed work. The scent of salt water drew him to the harbor. He walked through the streets of the city, hitched rides with the truck drivers. But he was careful not to spend too much time recalling what he had left for fear he might lose the dreams that kept him alive. He'd take to the road and try to hitch a ride to a better future.

His hope rose when a truck driver, a man who wore a short-brimmed denim cap and a smile that only worked on half his face, pulled over.

"I'm headed to Ocean City," the man said. "Where, young man, are you going?"

The thought of a city so bold and marvelous that it would take the name of the ocean itself sent his mind reeling.

"That's where I'm going, too," said young Stovec.

The driver must have read the boy's travails in his face, sensed them in the clothing that reeked of sweat and boxcars and the open road. His half-smile appeared again, and he nodded with an understanding that filled the boy's lungs like a breath of oxygen to a climber on a mountaintop.

"How lucky for you," he said. "Hop in."

He would never forget that first wide view of the Atlantic Ocean near the town of Rehoboth, Delaware. The ocean broke abruptly from the land and headed into endlessness. That day, it took on a cloudy emerald tint that would imprint itself forever in his memory. Even many years later, when he had seen the sea take on the otherworldly colors of splendid jewels, the look of the Atlantic that autumn day would remain his archetypal sea.

The autumn season still attracted visitors and the many who owned resort homes. And though swimming was left now to the daring few who took pleasure in challenging the cold, many still walked the beaches for health and to lose their troubles in the emptiness of the ocean. Some collected shells and scoured the sands for the remains of creatures that the sea had once swallowed and now spewed.

Chester's Seafood House, a square two-story restaurant overlooking the Atlantic, hired Phillip. The name had made him comfortable, and he took pride in his first real job as a busboy. The hand of destiny must have been at work to give him a job in such a marvelous location, he thought. The students who had bused the tables that summer had returned to school. The owner took kindly to young Stovec and helped him file his social security application. For the remainder of his business life, he would be "Stover" when the error on the social security application gave him his new identity.

A growth spurt came that winter and continued through the following spring. His neck thickened, and his frame began to fill with muscle, too. He had lied about his age by several years, but with his new growth, and the confidence that came with the life that had opened to him, he appeared older even than the 21 years he had given himself.

Stover would work at the restaurant for two years and become indispensable. The owner taught him how to become a successful businessman. Phillip learned well, and, at night, when he wasn't reading, he crafted his own business plans.

His dreams grew, became more vivid and detailed until he could see them come to fruition in his mind's eye like a glimpse of a distant ship coming ever closer to port. So it was not long before Phillip Stover, with the money he had diligently saved and some help from the restaurant owner, purchased a truck in surprisingly good condition. With it, he delivered the restaurant's marvelous crab cakes to other restaurants in Newark and Philadelphia and many stops along the way.

And that was just the beginning.

By the time he could legally purchase his first glass of alcohol, Phillip Stover owned three buildings and two thriving businesses. Those numbers would multiply in the coming years. He was a young man of rare vision, and he saw opportunities where others saw only barriers, if they saw anything at all. He added trucks and drivers to the seafood business, anchored by the crab cakes but later including shrimp and lobster and breaded fish fillets, and even an assortment of frozen vegetable products. With the freedom the drivers afforded him, he returned to school in the evenings, met his high school requirements, and moved seamlessly into college credits. His appetite for learning was insatiable, and he devoured books by lamplight to satisfy his yearning.

Still, he had yet to cross the ocean and answer his deepest dreams. That started to change when he secured an interesting business opportunity in the Caribbean when he was 30 years old, then another one in Europe a year later. He made the most of his trips by frequenting museums and art galleries, and by touring places he had yearned to visit and meeting, when he could, with learned men.

"What drove you?" I asked him as we settled down at his villa overlooking Hathaway Bay. The hillside setting afforded us a spectacular view of the water. Homes seemed carved out of the cliffs. Across from us, hills tapered to a point where the bay opened to the sea.

When he had suggested I join him at his villa, I should have expected no less glamorous a perch for Phillip Stover. We had continued our conversation during the hour-long drive, pausing frequently to enjoy the changing landscape as we neared the sea.

"What drove me? What energized me?" He paused. "I've thought about that often. Knowing what motivates a man gives one hope of replicating his success, I guess. A lot of folks – several reporters, in fact – have painted me as a man who saw the ugliest side of poverty and survived traumatic abuse. I've been portrayed as the tough son, who hated his lowly condition, vowed to become a rich man, and, somehow, made it to the summit of the American Dream."

He drank from a glass of mineral water and stared out at the bay. The wake of a pleasure boat cut a neat arc toward the mouth.

"But it wasn't the American Dream that drove me – at least not the money hunt that many perceive that dream to be. My dreams were fueled by something else. Passion. You see, most of what I did, I loved doing. Everything of any consequence that I've accomplished came doing something that I did with heart and passion.

"And," he continued, "when I pursued my passion, I found something worth more than money. I found my happiness."

Passion! Was there a word in our language with more power, any word possessed of so potent a mix of the sacred and the profane?

If passion was the key to Stover's happiness and success, I needed to understand it better.

Phillip summarized his perspective in three simple sentences.

"Passion is fire. Fire is heat. Heat produces change."

I struggled to absorb his message.

"Nothing accelerates change faster than heat," he went on. "We acknowledge that fact in the language, in metaphor. To 'turn up the heat' means to put on pressure, to make things happen.

"True, passion is an invisible fire that is as capable of consuming its possessor as obsession, lust or greed," he went on. "But its power is also capable of motivating and driving action.

"There is no force in all of nature more powerful than passion. If we could penetrate to the core of creation, I suspect we would find a bundle of energy burning with desire to be!"

I liked this poetic side of Stover, but he would not hang on this precipice of abstraction for long. His genius was in bringing ideas into reality.

"There's a very pragmatic dimension to passion," he said, abruptly switching gears. "What keeps men and women from living their dreams? Fear. Fear and lack of faith. They don't believe they can achieve what their heart desires most. Or they are afraid of leaving the comfortable confines of the here and now.

"But when passion fuels our engine, fear recedes into the background. Obstacles cease to be huge barriers."

We looked out on the water. It must have been several minutes before Stover interrupted the silence. "Passion may be the most conspicuous trait of happy people," he observed. Despite the stereotype of the dispassionate businessman, he felt that passion was the defining trait of most successful people. They see opportunities where others find only reasons they will fail and fall along the way.

"When you get down to it," he summarized, "my success in life – and not just in business – has come from saying 'Yes' to possibilities more than I have said 'No.'"

Over the next two hours, Stover shared examples of housewives, artists, and laborers he knew with uncommon passion for their work, their families, their causes, their hobbies, and life itself.

"If you live for money and you lose it, you have lost everything," he said. "But if a person is passionate about his or her life, you can take away all they own, and they still have their passion."

My afternoon in conversation with Phillip Stover was fascinating on many levels. He was not the cold model of efficiency, not the money machine I had imagined. He was a man of flesh and blood – blood that surged through him like some fiery river. I could see why others came to him so often to help jump start their charitable and business endeavors. Not for his money. And not just for his know-how. They wanted most to feel his fire, let it touch them and everything around them until they and the thing they sought had burst into fabulous flame.

"It's hard to believe you started out as a busboy in Ocean City," I said, shaking my head with admiration as his cook wheeled in a cart and doled out two late lunch plates.

"No," he said. "It really started in Baltimore. You can't imagine how much I loved those crab cakes. Bon appétit!"

And with that salute, we lifted our plates, adorned with crisp breaded crab cakes that melted in our mouth.

The afternoon sun had settled upon the bay, and yet our conversation had hardly slowed.

His stories and insights had lost none of their magic during the hours of our discussion. Each story reinforced Stover's fervent belief that the key to happiness isn't money. It's the passion that lets you enjoy every step of the journey. And the love you find along the way with your friends and family.

He then recalled the most important trip he had ever taken. "I had traveled all around the world. Yet there was one journey I had not yet dared to make – the journey back to my home."

Stover's first letters, which he had written about six months after his fight with his brother, went unanswered. He tried again a year later with the same result. By the time he finally heard from one of his sisters, Louise, years later, his mother and father had both passed away.

"Louise said they all were thrilled to tears to hear that I was alive and well and wondered why I had not written all these years. I knew then that Stanley must have intercepted my letters."

More than a year of correspondence passed between them before they planned their reunion. Louise had asked about his work in several letters, and he had mentioned only that he was involved in business. He had said little that would give them any indication of his remarkable success and wealth.

His return would entail many surprises.

The reunion took place at Louise's house. All of his sisters were there, as were two of his brothers. Tears flowed freely as they each embraced each other. They moved into the small kitchen.

"We were toasting my return and our glorious gathering," Phillip went on. "I had not dared to dampen our high spirits with a question about Stanley, whom I had yet to see and whom no one had yet mentioned.

"Suddenly, there he was. Stanley stood under the arched entryway that separated the kitchen from the front room."

Everyone grew quiet.

"I looked for a limp as he took his first steps toward me. I was quietly relieved when I saw his even gait. He stopped three feet away. He looked world-weary and sported a small protruding belly. But his thick neck and shoulders reminded me of the man I saw in the mirror each morning.

He stared at me with a look I could not begin to decipher.

"'My brother, the dreamer,' he said. 'Welcome back to your home.' Then he swallowed me in a bear hug, and we cried in each other's arms."

The Socrates Smith Notebook

Conversation with Phillip Stover:
A lesson in Passion.

Stover seems to have found happiness by pursuing his passion. His wealth is almost a by-product of his having pursued his passion. Randy's passion is his music. How can I not let him follow his dream? Even if he never gets rich, he should be following his own path towards a fulfilling life.

"Nothing great was ever achieved without enthusiasm."
  - Ralph Waldo Emerson

"The crucial thing to live for is the sense of life in what you are doing. If that is not there, then you are living according to other people's notion of how life should be lived."
  - Joseph Campbell

"The high prize of life, the crowning glory of a man is to be born with a bias to some pursuit which finds him in employment and happiness - whether it be to make baskets, or broadswords, or canals, or statues, or songs."
    - Ralph Waldo Emerson

"Lord, grant that I may always desire more than I can accomplish."
    - Michelangelo

"As I grow to understand life less and less, I learn to live it more and more."
    - Jules Renard

"I have found that the best way to give advice to your children is to find out what they want, and then advise them to do it."
    - Harry S. Truman

"The quality of a man's life is in direct proportion to his commitment to excellence, regardless of his chosen field of endeavor."
- Vince Lombardi

"If a man has any brains at all, let him hold on to his calling, and, in the grand sweep of things, his turn will come at last."
- William McCune

"It is not in doing what you like, but in liking what you do that is the secret to happiness."
- James Barrie

"A man can succeed at almost anything for which he has unlimited enthusiasm."
- Charles Schwab

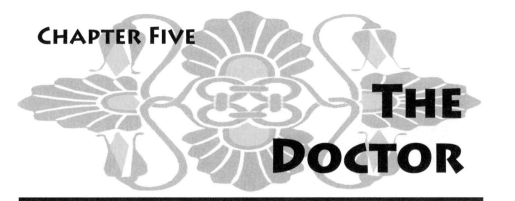

CHAPTER FIVE

THE DOCTOR

"**S**o tell me. How did it go?" Carrie asked at breakfast. I shared the highlights of my day with Phillip Stover. She listened to my summary of Stover's climb to success, and to my glowing assessment of this most thoughtful and fascinating man.

"What did he say about work?" she asked.

"Work?"

"You know. A job. Employment. Activity that brings in money to pay mortgages and light bills and stuff like that."

"It didn't come up," I said awkwardly.

"And you didn't *ask?*" she added. She shuffled to the sink and began cleaning the handful of dishes left from her dinner with the boys. The air was thick with unasked questions.

How could I convey the value of our meeting? How could I even broach the topic of the Code to Happiness? How ironic that my pursuit of happiness was producing the bad vibrations I was now feeling from my wife!

"It didn't seem appropriate," I said, without explanation. Then I added: "We'll have other opportunities to talk business."

Carrie hung the dishtowel on the stove handle, patted me on the shoulder in a way that conveyed more patience than understanding, and left the room.

My wife knew how to make her point.

I spent all day and part of the evening making phone calls and setting up job interviews. I was optimistic that something interesting would open up. Hopefully soon, I thought, looking at the bills piled upon my desk.

I must have been anxious because I found it difficult to sleep that night. Restless and wide awake, I got out of bed. The clock read 4:30 AM. I put on my bathrobe and headed to my library, a small room that served as my office and reading area.

Spirits loomed large in the modest chamber. I had built its shelves a number of summers ago. Books climbed clear to the ceiling. The authors' voices seemed to whisper from the leather-bound volumes. The words and wisdom of great minds came back to me across the centuries like the murmurs of a midnight breeze. How often had they challenged or nourished or enlightened me? How often had these spirits uncannily found my open ear when I needed his or her message most?

I read the spines of books by the great philosophers – from old classics by Plato and Aristotle to several modern authors – who found new and compelling ways to describe the human condition, which, it occurred to me, had changed little over the centuries. My reverie broke abruptly with a click and shuffle at our back door. Silence followed. More sound. I heard the tinkling of keys.

I walked down the hallway to the kitchen and flipped on a light. There, in a sweatshirt rumpled by a long night's drive, her long, shiny hair falling neatly from a white baseball cap, was my daughter.

"Hello, Dad," said Ellen.

I crossed the room and hugged her. She clung to me like a tired and frightened child.

The household awakened. First, Carrie arrived in her robe, as surprised as I was at Ellen's sudden appearance. Then came Eddie, for once out of bed without our prodding. Finally, our resident rock star, wearing only bib blue jeans and a two-day beard, poked his head in.

"What's all the racket?" Randy called from the doorway. The sight of Ellen brought a rare early morning grin. "Hey, Sis!"

The house was soon bustling with coffee and breakfast and chatter, and whatever gloom had carried my daughter through our back door temporarily vanished amid the marvelous tumult of reunited Smiths.

We let Ellen bask in the noise and attention from the family. It took Eddie's bluntness to put the question on the table.

"Why are you here, El? Something wrong?"

Ellen nodded her head. "I wanted to see Grandpa."

I suspected there was more to the story but didn't ask. There'd be time for that.

"You must have left at two in the morning," said Randy, stuffing down a doughnut. "Man, you keep worse hours than I do."

Ellen ignored the remark.

"How's Grandpa doing?"

I tried to lighten the mood. "I don't know what to believe. The doctor thinks he's fading fast. Your grandfather is planning his next fishing trip."

Eddie piped in. "I'll put my money on Grandpa Abe."

Carrie and I exchanged glances. She smiled faintly.

I got more of the story when Ellen and I drove to the hospital an hour later. Aside from wanting to see her grandfather, it seemed that she also needed to get away from her college environment and its chronic stress and inescapable pressures. A thoughtless roommate with an annoying boyfriend. Ellen was disappointed in the way her relationship with Nick, her own boyfriend, was going. On top of that, she was now having second thoughts about her major. The list of negatives was long.

"Ellen," I said. "Somewhere along the line, you're going to need a new pair of glasses."

"What do you mean?" she asked.

"You see an awful lot of gloom," I said.

"I can't help it. That's the way things are," she said, irritated at my insensitivity and lack of understanding.

"Maybe you're missing something," I said. "Maybe a different outlook is in order. I'm sure you can find something positive to focus upon." I thought about my dad. "Something to appreciate."

Ellen grew quiet and stared across the dashboard.

"What is this place?" asked Ellen.

The DΣLPHI was hopping again. George held the door and gushed with warm greeting as I introduce him to Ellen.

Ellen looked surprised at the bustle of activity and George's ever-changing mix of quaint charm and tawdry attempts at elegance and sophistication. He had just taped a travel poster to the window. It promoted tours to Athens and featured the Parthenon with the tagline: "Western civilization, welcome home!"

"Dad, what *is* this place?" Ellen murmured again.

"It's my hangout," I said jokingly. "Hey, you're in college. You know the importance of a hangout."

"My only hangout lately is the library."

I ignored her comment. Sometimes it's better not to say anything.

We found a table. Ellen studied the odd blend of people, walls, and décor that now represented the closest thing I had to an office.

I poked around for relevant topics that I hoped would distract Ellen from the sadness that she wore all over her face. The prospect of seeing her grandfather in the hospital was obviously weighing her down. But she was reluctant to elaborate on any of the matters I broached. She could shut up like a clam without any warning. Finally, I simply stopped trying. She was tired and stressed. Maybe stopping at the DƩLPHI had not been such a great idea after all.

"Oh, my God. She's her father's clone!" Our mugs had filled almost magically. Sophie stood beside the table, unabashedly studying Ellen as if she were a framed photograph. "No, not really," Sophie reassessed, biting her knuckle. "She has her mother's eyes. The shape of her face, too."

She was right, of course, eerily right. I could see surprise on Ellen's face, wondering just what connection Sophie had shared with her deceased mother. But before she could formulate the question, Sophie had the conversation running in another direction.

"What's the matter?" asked Sophie as Ellen sat dumbfounded. "Oh. Right. You don't drink coffee. Sorry about that." She mopped the coffee blobs from around Ellen's mug, but left the full mug before her.

"She's a beautiful girl, Socrates," said Sophie, nodding to indicate to another table that she would be right there – in her good time. Ellen grabbed my sleeve and silently mouthed a one-word inquiry: "Socrates?" I just spread my hands and shrugged.

"I know the two of you don't have much time," said Sophie. She looked at Ellen. "You're going to visit your grandpa, huh? I'm sure he'll enjoy the visit." Sophie put her hand on my shoulder and squeezed. She leaned over. I noticed a strange, wonderful fragrance, more like incense than perfume, emanating from her.

She whispered in my ear. "You ought to see a doctor there, too," she said before spinning away suddenly.

"Doc Bradshaw?" I called.

"No," she said, as she buzzed off to the next table. "Ortiz!" She shouted back over her shoulder

"Ortiz?" I said, to no avail.

"Dad, whooo is *that*?!!" asked Ellen, not sure whether she should be amused or totally appalled.

"That, my dear, is Sophie, Oracle of the DΣLPHI Café," I said, raising my eyebrows in mock mystery.

"How would she know about Mom or that I resemble her?"

"I told you. She's an oracle. All-seeing, all-knowing," I said.

"Right!" said Ellen. She could not take her eyes off of Sophie, floating from table to table and darting back and forth from the kitchen.

The sight of the hospital made Ellen uneasy.

"Relax," I said. "Grandpa's in good spirits."

I hoped that was still the case.

I poked my head through the door to hedge my bet. Dad looked worn and raggedy, but he lit up like a light bulb at the sight of Ellen.

"Hi, Grandpa," she said, almost running across the room into his thin arms. They hugged for a long time during which Grandpa Abe whispered in Ellen's ear in a voice too soft for me to distinguish the words.

Dad and I exchanged a few words, but his attention was not with me. I excused myself and headed down the corridor.

I caught Bradshaw between hospital rounds. The only encouraging part of his update was that Dad was comfortable. Apparently, Dad had little going for him but hope and attitude.

My father was smiling and talking louder than I had heard him in some time when I returned to the room. So was Ellen, to my delight.

"Son, take your worried brow for a long walk. I need more time with my grand-daughter," he said. Then he turned to Ellen. "Your old man worries too much. Did anyone ever tell him that?"

"I think it runs in the family, Grandpa," she said with a grin that brightened the room.

I chose to ignore the comments. "I'll leave you two alone again," I said.

The hospital bustled at mid-morning. I took a shortcut down a set of stairs that I thought led to the snack bar. Instead, I found myself in the hospital's new research wing. In contrast with the drab utility of its exterior design, the hospital's interior was light and airy and alive with monuments to medical science. Several displays commemorated patrons of healing and landmarks in medical research. Another display case marked highlights in American health research, listing the work at Hoppe among the latest in a long line of marvelous contributions to mankind's knowledge of human health. I admired a bust of Hippocrates and read a short article on nutrition that hung from a pegboard. It had been written by one of the staff physicians for a prominent medical journal. I paused at another wall plaque that quoted the founder of the hospital. He had been one of the most famous physicians in the country decades earlier. The plaque read:

> ## "GOOD HEALTH IS THE FOUNDATION FOR A GOOD LIFE."
> ## - EDMUND J. HOPPE

I continued walking down the hallway when a nameplate on an office door stopped me in my tracks:

> ## JULIA M. ORTIZ, M.D., DIRECTOR,
> ## THE HOPPE INSTITUTE FOR MIND-BODY RESEARCH

I read the name again. Ortiz. That was the name Sophie had dropped at the DƐLPHI. I wondered whether this was the doctor she was referring to. I decided to take my chances and stop in to introduce myself.

The office door had been left ajar. I pushed it open halfway and called "Hello." No one answered. I knocked and peered into the office through the open door. Several models of the human brain were set on the deep cherry wood shelves. A skeleton wearing that familiar Halloween grin stood in a corner.

I was intrigued and vowed to return to visit Dr. Ortiz.

I turned to leave and found myself face-to-face with a gelatinous mass of tissue, moist and glistening, and, in a cold rush of recognition, looking every bit like a human brain.

"Whoa," I said, taking an awkward and hurried step backward.

The brain moved suddenly to chest level, and there stood a tall, attractive woman with shoulder-length, reddish-blonde hair pulled back into a neat ponytail.

"Is that real?" I asked, regaining my bearings.

"No, I'm afraid not," she said with a laugh.

"Good. I'm glad."

"It's quite a good reproduction though, isn't it?" she asked.

"Yes, it certainly is," I said. "Not that I'm well acquainted with uncapped human brains, mind you. But, yes, it's quite impressive, very convincing."

"Thank you, Mr...."

"Smith," I said.

Her forehead furled. Dad was right. The Smith name was such a cliché that it sometimes challenged belief.

"I'm Dr. Ortiz," she said. "How can I help you?"

"I was just passing by," I fumbled. "I thought you might help me. You see, a friend, Sophie, mentioned you this morning in passing. Then I saw your name on the door. I just thought I'd stop in."

She puzzled over my mention of Sophie. I ignored her reaction and pushed on.

"As I look around at the exhibits, I'm finding myself intrigued. I'm curious whether medical research can help me with a project I'm working on."

"Oh," she replied. "What's your project?"

"Happiness."

She looked at me and smiled. "Happiness. That's interesting. I think our research might be useful to you. Our current studies are focusing on the relationship between a healthy lifestyle and mental health. There is compelling evidence that lifestyle is clearly linked to happiness and a sense of well-being." She paused. "And Sophie suggested you look me up," she said with a twinkle in her eye. "How it all fits with happiness...that's very interesting."

"I'm anxious to hear about your studies," I said.

Dr. Ortiz studied me again. Her index finger tapped the tray. Yes, it really did look like a human brain. "I have a meeting later this afternoon," she said with a smile. "But I can spare a few minutes now."

"Almost everyone can lead a healthier – and happier – life," began Dr. Ortiz. "Scientific research has established that proposition."

We were seated in her office, on either side of her massive mahogany desk. Her manner reminded me of a college professor, and she mentioned that she had once considered a life in the classroom before she had embarked on a research career.

She touched on some of the highlights of her earlier work, including studies on diet, sleep, exercise, and family history. Her current work involved studies of brain activity. "My research associates have teamed up with scientists to work with patients who have been admitted for the treatment of psychological disorders," she said. "But the premise of our study is not simply to find a better treatment for these disorders. It's to flip the classic approach to medical care on its head. We want to learn not just how to treat diseases but also to provide guidelines that promote wellness and enhance our quality of life. In recent years, we have benefited from important new research studies and new technology, which gives us a new way to view activity in the human brain. Viewing the brain activity of both optimistic individuals and those suffering from depression has revealed major differences in the brain's function. At the risk of oversimplifying the matter, those who see the rosy side of life – the so-called optimists – have elevated activity on the left side. Those with a dreary outlook have more elevated activity on the right side. Some scientists are now convinced that it's even possible," she paused, "to *think* your way into being more positive, more optimistic – happier."

Dr. Ortiz believed that this research was vitally important in light of an increasing trend by many doctors to use drugs to alter mood and behavior. I agreed, wondering if this quick-fix age had any interest in the rewards of what we once called "the good life."

"We are not just victims of our circumstances and genetics. We are not puppets controlled by our upbringing," Ortiz stated emphatically. "We can make choices that positively change our feeling about ourselves, our circumstances, and the world around us. Scientific evidence is demonstrating that we can consciously choose to become healthier and happier."

She showed me images that represented some of this cutting edge research. I was out of my element in her realm of brain images and models. But from what I could see – what I was told, to be more accurate – the images reflected varying degrees of activity in portions of the brain during contrasting states of calm and distress.

"Our most interesting findings suggest that through a conscious, well-reasoned, well-executed plan of self-therapy, people are able to minimize or eliminate the patterns in their brains created by stress or pessimism and replace them with patterns that are found in optimistic people's brains. This is a powerful finding with huge implications. Certainly, the drugs currently used to treat depression and assist those with behavioral disorders have an important place. But not everyone is doomed to a life of unhappiness without drugs. Modern science is proving that most of us can think – and act – our way to a happier life."

Ortiz walked over to the smiling skeleton model. She put her right arm around its shoulders as if posing for a photograph with a dear friend. Suddenly, Mr. Bones tipped the top of his skull as if he were doffing his cap. Dr. Ortiz grabbed a marker from her flip chart and pointed to the exposed brain within the cranium.

"When science began brain imaging, the bulk of our observations in the research labs were of brains in states of turmoil," said Dr. Ortiz. "Electro-shock therapy has been used as a means of 'settling' the agitated brain by sending a charge of electricity through the skull and into the brain. Medical science has invested a lot of time, money, and energy in developing drugs that directly act upon the agitated sections of the brain. Today, we spend billions of dollars on such drugs in this country alone. These deliver quick relief, though with varying degrees of long-term effectiveness. Unfortunately, too many people seek to find happiness from a pill. Current research suggests that the types of brain changes observed in patients who have been administered drugs can be replicated with a change of outlook and perspective. More importantly, changes in perspective are longer lasting and, potentially, even more effective."

"And what about other health practices?" I asked. "Does a healthy lifestyle make us happier?"

"Great question! Actually, a healthy lifestyle is a very important component of happiness," said Dr. Ortiz. "A healthy lifestyle not only helps to minimize unnecessary pain and worries but increases our capacity to enjoy life as well. Leading a healthy lifestyle can do wonders for us."

"Can you be a little clearer? What particular lifestyle choices can help us to enjoy life more fully?"

But before Dr. Ortiz could answer, the phone rang. She was needed. I thanked her for her time and apologized again for my intrusion.

"No trouble at all," she said. A thought struck her. "In fact…follow me," she said, leading me down the hallway to a small library. "There are racks of materials here you may find interesting. I'm sorry I can't lend them to you, but you are certainly welcome to stay and read anything you find interesting." I thanked her profusely as she hurried away.

In the middle of her desk sat a bulging nut-brown three-ring binder. I hesitated before opening it; the sheer size of the volume was intimidating. I began to leaf through it. A plasticine sheet held the title page: *Health and Healthy Outlook* by Dr. Julia M. Ortiz. I pored through it swiftly to gain a sense of its contents. A mix of printed and handwritten text alternated with articles, computer-generated charts, photographs, and graphics that had been carefully removed from the pages of scientific journals with a surgeon's skill. Yellow Post-it notes with brief references flagged numerous pages. The doctor's observations and commentary appeared in red ink on the journal reports.

I opened to a blue index tab, "Understanding mood enhancement," and began to read.

Many of the scientific terms used in the text defied my layman's comprehension until I hit a section entitled "Simple Steps toward Health and Healthy Outlook."

The style shifted from the formal scientific jargon of her earlier notes to pragmatic, straightforward advice on how our habits and activities affected health. Lifestyle and behavior stimulated parts of the brain associated with our mood, it said. I took detailed notes. Science had taken our understanding of the mind-body connection to new levels. Factors such as diet, sleep, exercise, and exposure to sunlight all factored into, and could directly affect, our mood. I took copious notes so I could include these points later that evening in my own notebook. The relationship between a healthy lifestyle and a healthy outlook on life appeared much stronger than I had previously realized.

I turned the pages, fully engrossed, for nearly an hour. My thoughts returned to Dad and Ellen when I heard the loudspeaker page Dr. Bradshaw. I was finding the new research projects exciting and vowed to learn more. But now, it was time to check on my father and daughter.

Our home looked warm and inviting as Ellen and I pulled in the drive. Carrie was outside, watering her late-season flowers. Her gloves were black and damp from garden work. The hose dripped from the base of the nozzle connection. I promised myself I would replace the washer the next day.

"Hi, you two!" Carrie said, walking over to us and giving us both a big hug. "How did it go?"

"It was great to see Grandpa Abe. He told me the funniest joke I've heard in a long time!" It was nice to see Ellen with a hint of a smile. Carrie and I looked at each other in silent recognition. We were both pleased to see even a small improvement in her mood. Being around my dad, with his upbeat mood, had been good for Ellen. Perhaps, I thought to myself, something as simple as surrounding yourself with positive people carried you closer to happiness.

Autumn filled my senses with its contrary themes of death and beauty. Carrie and Ellen had gone inside, and I was left alone in the yard. I grabbed the rake that was leaning against the house. The maples blazed in a brilliant display of late season color. The leaves delivered a faint, acrid odor cut by the heady rush of cool autumn air. In the waning light, puffy white clouds highlighted the late afternoon sky.

My head buzzed with recollection of the day's discussions as I raked. My shoulders and back ached for activity, and I realized how little I had exercised since I had embarked on the quest for the Code. Vaguely, I recalled my laps at the gym and the rushed workout that had ended with a couple of quick rounds pummeling the big bag. That was too long ago. My diet hadn't been great, either. I had been mostly grabbing sandwiches and coffee on the run.

If there was one thing my time with Dr. Ortiz had made clear, it was the fact that my own search for happiness would require more than just adopting the right attitude. I had to take action as well. Maybe adopting a healthy lifestyle was the most important action one could take. Good health not only cleared major barriers to happiness, it also enhanced vitality and a sense of well-being.

Would I ever crack the Code to Happiness? Who knew? But at least I could adopt a healthier lifestyle. A lifestyle that included a good diet, exercise, and sleep seemed central to any search for happiness. I'd look over my notes from Dr. Ortiz's office later and see what else I could do.

I was interrupted by the sounds of leaves crackling beneath the wheels of a blue Oldsmobile Cutlass. It stopped abruptly at the driveway. Eddie spilled out of the back seat, backpack and football in tow. We both waved to the driver as the car sped away.

"How was practice?" I asked.

"Pretty good," he said. "Too many dropped passes, though. Coach doesn't think we're ready for Carter yet. But I think we'll kill 'em."

"They went to the state quarterfinals last year and have one of the top defenses in the state," I warned. "They're a team to be reckoned with."

"Go deep, Dad," Eddie said, oblivious to my words of caution. He dropped his pack and felt for the laces of the oblong leather. The rake dropped into my pile of leaves, and I broke long across our lawn and the neighbor's. Recent inactivity gnawed at my thighs, and the kinks in my back and shoulders crackled as I tried to conjure a burst of speed. Eddie uncorked a beauty. I was surprised at how quickly it arrived over my right shoulder and into my waiting hands. I tucked it away and crossed the imaginary goal line, flush with resuscitated pride and the joy of pure physical function.

"Way to go, Dad!" shouted Eddie.

"If you throw like that this weekend, Carter Academy can call it quits after the first quarter," I said.

I jogged back and snapped an underhand pass back at Eddie, suddenly realizing how heavily I was panting.

"You OK, Dad?" asked Eddie.

"Yeah. Just a little out of shape," I confessed, with a cough and a laugh. "But not for long! Your coach may even want me to suit up soon."

"Right, Dad." Eddie was not amused.

The Socrates Smith Notebook

Conversation with Dr. Julia Ortiz:
A lesson in healthy lifestyles.

My day at the hospital was not what I expected.
But I came away with sound advice on how to
improve health and, perhaps, happiness. Ideas to
follow up on include:

1. Exercise.

2. Sunlight. Our innate love of sunny days and blue skies
has a biological basis. Sunlight contributes
significantly to a sense of well-being.

3. Practice relaxing through meditation, breathing, and
other techniques.

4. Sleep. Getting sufficient sleep improves memory,
alertness, mental acuity, and motivation and enhances
our sense of joy and fullness of living.

5. Laughter. Nothing can boost outlook and mood like a healthy dose of humor. To be able to find humor in life's frustrations, hurts, and unfortunate surprises is one of the best means of meeting its challenges. Indulging in light, even silly humor can reduce the weight of one's psychic burden.

6. Diet. Improving health and appearance may boost self-esteem and generate confidence and a healthy love and appreciation for life.

"He who has health has hope, and he who has hope has everything."
  - Arabian proverb

"A healthy body is a guest-chamber for the soul; a sick body is a prison."
  -Francis Bacon

"Protect your health. Without it you face a serious handicap for success and happiness."
  -Harry Banks

"Those who do not find time for exercise will have to find time for illness."
　　- Earl of Derby

"To preserve health is a moral and religious duty, for health is the basis of all social virtues. We can no longer be useful when not well."
　　- Samuel Johnson

"Never hurry; take plenty of exercise; always be cheerful, and take all the sleep you need, and you may expect to be well."
　　- James Clarke

"It better befits a man to laugh at life than to lament over it."
　　- Seneca

CHAPTER SIX

THE PSYCHOLOGIST

"Pretty good," I said. Sophie had poured me a fresh cup of George's latest blend, a powerful, exotic aroma I associated with a tropical forest.

Her hand fluttered. "It ain't that bad," she said.

"So how did you know?" I asked.

"Know what?"

"You know…Ellen's resemblance to my first wife. I don't recall your ever having met her."

"Boy, you're easy to impress," she said with such nonchalance that I knew that any further pursuit of the matter would be futile.

She wiped the counter with purpose and elbow grease, went back over it with a dry towel. Then she tossed the cloth beneath the counter and stood challengingly before me.

"So, what have you learned?" she asked.

"Learned? About the Code?" I said. "Well, I'm not sure. I've had several fascinating meetings and conversations recently. With Stover, Dr. Ortiz, Rube. Even with my dad. I know their messages are related to happiness, but I can't figure out how they fit together into a code." I searched Sophie's face for a response, but found none. "The truth is, these days I can't tell where my life stops and this quest for the Code starts."

She topped off my mug and flashed a look that, for a moment, seemed to say that I was not the student, not the pilgrim she had hoped I would be.

"Must you separate them?" she asked.

I brushed off her remark.

"Look. This Code to Happiness means a lot to me. But I'm not Socrates, and this is not ancient Athens," I blurted. "I can't just wander the countryside and the city streets engaging people in philosophical discussion. If this search is real, I'd like to press ahead and solve it. Solve it now!"

My speech seemed petulant, and I felt suddenly hollow and out of character. "The truth is, I could use your help. More help, that is."

"I think you need to see a psychologist," she said.

"Thanks for the suggestion," I muttered with a trace of embarrassment. "Sorry for jumping at you."

"Is that what you were doing?" she asked. "Shame on you…But forget the apology. I was being serious."

"Serious? That I need a shrink?"

"Well," she said with a smile. "You need to see this one."

"What does the psychologist have to offer?" I asked, suddenly sensing I was back in the hunt.

"Patience," she said.

"OK, OK," I said. "I'm trying."

"We live in fast times," explained Dr. Frederick Frolich, my gracious new host. We stood side by side at the window.

"Yes, we do," I agreed as we paused to take in the view. "The modern man's lament. There's never enough time!"

His office overlooked our city's broad and majestic river which rolled inexorably, breaking around the pylons as it made its way to the Lake. Several recreational boats were taking advantage of the balmy Indian Summer day. On the far side, a barge glided, with slow and effortless purpose.

"Funny. The pace doesn't seem so fast from up here," I said.

Dr. Frolich agreed. "Without a little time to make sense of things, our pace can eat us up. We are so focused on getting through the day that we let the hours slip right through our fingers like tiny grains of sand."

"It's easy to get caught up in a hundred needs and a thousand distractions," I agreed.

"The problem," Frolich replied, "is that we often move too fast and eat ourselves up along the way. We want so much. We think we need so much. What's worse, we think we need it all right now."

His smile and manner radiated warmth, and I felt very much at home in his office.

"Yes. Instant gratification is the curse of our convenience world," Frolich continued. "We want every outcome determined immediately, every desire fulfilled right *now*. We lose the capacity to let life unfold."

"And it seems that lost patience diminishes our capacity for happiness," I said, thinking about my own impatience as a parent, spouse, businessman and, more recently, in my rush to discover the Code.

"It certainly can," he said.

Frolich explained that we are too often afraid that any want or need we can't satisfy right now will go unfulfilled, that any uncomfortable situation or disappointment which can't be changed with the click of the computer mouse or clang of a cash register is too much to bear.

"I sense sometimes that too many of us believe that family, friends, and even the government are responsible for our happiness," I suggested. "That they are responsible for taking care of our problems and concerns."

"Yes," he said. "And, ironically, the more we blame others for our problems, the less they are likely to help us, or for that matter, even want to help us. We create barriers that alienate others, and ironically, only exacerbate our unhappiness. If we could just learn to be more patient – with ourselves and with others…" His voice trailed off.

I thought about the women and men whom I regarded as happy and productive. Most of them – even those I regarded as energetic and persistent – had a certain hard-to-describe serenity. They did not seem to live in fear of the "what ifs" or worry about the possible unpleasant outcome of future events. They allowed life to flow, like the river outside our window. People like Stover and Rube and Dr. Ortiz, while obviously individuals who were quick to take action when warranted, acknowledged that, like fine wine, some things can only come to fruition when they are ready. I thought of my dad, who could sit quietly waiting for a single fish to bite at the end of his line. Now that was an exercise in patience!

The messages of my recent mentors came to me in slow waves. In retrospect, each of their lessons seemed to carry patience as a subtext. Dr. Ortiz's message of good health made no mention of crash diets or miracle foods that transformed men and women into super-beings. Hers was a lifestyle message that offered enduring benefit through prolonged, *patient* practice.

And what of Rube's story? If Rube, or anyone else for that matter, changed interests every day without ever acquiring a satisfying level of expertise, how rewarding could that possibly be? Perhaps the fresh curiosity that keeps us young needs to be complemented by a measure of persistence. And wasn't persistence merely one form of patience?

Events may develop slowly or rapidly. Often, the timing defies our control. Ironically, the more we try to control them, the less control we have.

"Wisdom," Frolich observed, "comes from recognizing the difference between events we can control and those we cannot."

"I have the Serenity Prayer framed on my wall at home," I nodded. "'God, grant me the serenity to accept the things I cannot change, the courage to change the things I can, and the wisdom to know the difference.'"

But I hadn't yet heard the most interesting part of Dr. Frolich's story.

New York, New York! The city was in his blood the moment he arrived at Grand Central Station and lugged his overstuffed suitcase to a cabby's open trunk.

Frolich had left a safe, protected existence in Bertha, Ohio, for life in the Big Apple. Immediately, he fell in love with the city and its street vendors, hustlers, hard-jawed men, sharp-tongued women, and strident children. The world was a more curious and far more demanding place than he had ever known. The people on the New York streets flashed different faces than those he had seen in the "how-are-ya" towns he had grown up in. The city was a cauldron bubbling over with emotion and energy that made each day fascinating.

Without a career foothold, Frolich grabbed work as he could. He filled in on a construction crew. He lugged rock in wheelbarrows and trucks, wrestling with air hammers that sent earth-shattering vibrations through his entire body. After a while, to help make ends meet, he took a job as a waiter at a small Greek diner.

He found New York women difficult to meet at first. His relative shyness had left him at a loss when they smiled in passing or feigned indifference. That changed when Frolich began to frequent the local sports bars with friends from his jobs. Soon, he had met a well-to-do young woman who gave him a glimpse of the wealth and lifestyle that gave New York City its glamour and mystique. One evening, she brought him to her apartment, and, from her window, they shared her stunning view of Manhattan. He decided then that he would do whatever it might take to share in the wealth and greatness he saw around him. He wanted it all.

And he wanted it now.

He became attracted to people with a knack for turning a quick dollar. Often illegally. Most of his acquaintances were increasingly tied to racetrack gambling, a few to illicit numbers games. Both held equal fascination.

At first, he allocated portions of his paycheck for "investment." But stock investment was a game of buy and hold that chafed against his restlessness. He needed the quick answers and the rapid return.

Soon he was in the thick of any game into which he could afford the ante, and a few that stretched beyond. He bet on basketball games, prizefights, and the race card at Pimlico. Early winnings fed his hopes of rapid wealth.

But the losses came, too. At first they only made the thrill of the next win that much more intense. But then his debts began to mount, and soon his paychecks were gone before they reached his hands.

And then, abruptly, his life changed one day. Frolich was riding a late night subway with a neighborhood friend, Lyle Peabody. Lyle would have preferred to watch a ballgame on TV, but Frolich had shamed him into joining him for a poker game in the north end of the city. The subway knocked and chugged and whined along the rails, grinding and squealing at each stop. The blurred signs and dark tunnel walls did little to dull his growing anxiety. How would he cover his gambling debts? His landlord, utilities, and other necessities already claimed most of his paycheck, and he wanted money in his pocket for the evenings, not to mention the next game of cards. So lost in thought was he that he barely noticed the pretty young lady in the knitted beret and red silk scarf seated across the aisle from him.

What happened next occurred so quickly that he would never be able to piece it all together.

The train squealed and groaned to a stop. The doors flipped open. A man with a navy blue ski mask and olive-green army jacket suddenly appeared at the door. He fired a shot. Until that moment, Frolich had not even noticed another man in a long charcoal overcoat. Now the man commanded attention as he bounced off the vertical handrail and fell to his knees. The masked man fired several more shots, stepped in quickly and yanked the briefcase from the man's grip.

Frolich watched the shooter race to the subway exit and toward the street.

Shrieks from panic-stricken commuters rose as the echoes of the gunshots faded. The man in the charcoal coat lay in a pool of dark blood, his face lifeless as a mannequin. It was only when a middle-aged black woman beside the door began to scream that Frolich saw that the shots had claimed a second victim. Against the screaming woman's shoulder rested the head of the young woman in the knitted beret.

And then he noticed a third victim.

Slumped quietly against the subway window was Lyle Peabody.

Brother Bernard sounded the bell in the faint first light of day. Bong. Bong... Six times the bell sounded with a low rich resonance that summoned the monastery to another day of work and prayer.

Frederick Frolich had found peace in his year at the monastery. After the subway massacre, the monks had taken him in as one of their own. There he had pulled the threads of his life together, woven them into something that began to resemble order, if not direction.

The fact that man could not hide from suffering even within the monastery walls became clear to Frolich barely two months after his arrival there. That was the day when Friar Albert, the venerable head of the priory, had passed away suddenly in his sleep. Frolich watched the monks mourn their beloved leader. They did not avoid his passing or make it into something foreign. Rather, they prayed for the repose of their leader's soul. And in granting death and suffering their place in the cycle of life, the monks robbed it of its stifling power. That conscious attention to their grief helped them to transcend their suffering until their spirits grew and grew, some days even seeming to touch that larger spirit to which they all prayed and aspired.

Frolich, who turned to the monastery after the railroad massacre in a desperate attempt to find meaning and renewed purpose, slowly began to reshape his life. Gradually, the anguish, doubt, and guilt that had haunted him since that fateful day on the subway had settled. Not disappeared, of course. That might never happen. But now he understood it in a different context – one based on the monastery's emphasis on forgiveness, love and compassion.

And the healing power of time.

Frolich learned many valuable lessons at the priory, even, with the gentle instruction of the monks, lessons from its garden. Isolated by a waist-high wall constructed of stones of varying earth tones, the garden offered timeless lessons about life. He learned from the vegetables and flowers in the garden and the trees in the nearby orchard that life was not something you controlled, was not a simple end product you stamped out of a machine with dead-on accuracy. In the garden, you planted seed, watered, extracted weeds, and hoped the plants would be favored by sufficient sunlight.

And you waited and watered.

Watered with purpose and waited.

Waited without guarantee but with hope.

With care and patience, the flowers and vegetables grew. Never all, of course. Some seeds were doomed by Nature. Some you destroyed through miscalculation or neglect. But most grew, and many flourished. And, in the end, patience was rewarded with beauty and bounty.

The monastery was a welcome respite and a place of peace. But it was not his home. Frolich would be leaving tomorrow. The monastery had taught him lessons about patience and suffering, but he also knew that its walls were a barrier between him and the people he needed once again to touch.

But this time he needed to touch them in a different way.

And so, with expressions of love and gratitude to Brother Bernard and the dozen other members of that pious community, he said his good-byes. He was heading back to New York. His hope of finding meaning burned like the candle he had lit in the monastery's chapel each day for Lyle Peabody's soul.

Frolich's new life would bring him new answers. He wanted to study psychology, to know what drives men and women to do what they do, what had caused him to make the choices that had brought him to this crossroads, and what made others despondent or even dangerous.

But beyond mere academic understanding, Frolich wanted to relieve the anguish of others.

He took an entrance exam and scored well, so well that he was given a scholarship that would largely fund his studies. He would fill in the rest with part-time jobs that would leave little time for relaxation and the pastimes that had plagued his past.

The textbooks were filled with answers, although, over time, Frolich learned not to blindly trust their sometimes too neatly categorized conclusions. He came to realize that hanging a name on a behavior did not qualify as wisdom. At times, psychology seemed as much of an art as a science, a discipline with many viewpoints but few certainties.

He found himself constantly thinking back to his past, to his upbringing and to those whom he had met at each juncture of his life, for better or for worse. Where his studies would take him, he was not certain. But a part of him felt sure his mission in life was to help others.

Frolich was a passionate student. He was up early, read scholarly books and journals over cups of strong coffee, attended classes, and met with his instructors. What free time he possessed he poured back into his studies, studying late into the night at the school library and attending lectures by men and women whose names dropped meaningfully from the mouths of his professors and peers.

He jumped at the chance to work at the Fox River Day Treatment Center following graduation. Fox River offered a structured life and daily treatment for adults, young and old, for whom life had proven too challenging and complicated. Most problems were connected to drug or alcohol abuse or depression. Frolich loved the work and loved the people.

His first patient was a young woman named Elizabeth Eaton, a young woman suffering from severe depression. Many of his colleagues were concerned that the Institute wasn't equipped to handle her needs. She had dangerous tendencies that made her a potential liability to the other patients, not to mention nervous members of the staff.

But they had all misjudged the power of Frolich's persistence, his patient trust that his efforts would ultimately bear fruit. They also misjudged the power of his approach. Rather than focus on the cause of his patient's depression, he concentrated on what made her happy and how she could learn to give more of her attention to *those* matters.

It was Frolich's first success, but not his last. His career had since been marked with similar success stories. Over time, he acquired a wonderful reputation as a member of the new school of positive psychology, designed to help his patients find – and focus on – their strengths and passions. Frolich had an extraordinary intuition, and his creative efforts to bring his patients well-being seemed to succeed far more than fail.

We had been engrossed in our conversation for some time. Finally, Frolich rose. I joined him at the window. The river flowed like a fluid melody with boats and buoys playing its theme. "You can't always gauge the impact of your work, or what you do in life, for that matter," he said. "At least not always right away."

"How's that?" I puzzled.

He smiled and pointed to a picture on his desk.

"Your wife?" I asked. He smiled and nodded his head.

A year ago, he had spoken to a large group of educators on the subject of appreciation. His theme was that some gifts, some lessons, might not be understood for years, maybe decades. There always remained, nevertheless, an opportunity to appreciate life today while patiently waiting for its lessons to reveal themselves later.

A number of attendees crowded the podium after his speech. One woman hung in the background, waiting patiently for the others to ask questions and extend their thanks. She was still there when the others had dispersed.

"I would like to thank you, too," she said. She was a tall woman, very pretty, with a confident, almost stately bearing. His eyes fixed intensely upon her.

"I'm glad you enjoyed the speech," he said.

"My appreciation goes well beyond your speech today," she said, smiling.

For a moment, tired from his speech and a long day, Frolich looked at her without recognition. And then, it struck him.

"Elizabeth Eaton!" he marveled, and suddenly he was the one bubbling over with questions and enthusiasm.

She had become an English teacher, gotten married, and was raising two school-aged children of her own. She spoke only minimally of herself, describing her children in loving detail, and then praising her students.

She became for a moment very serious, sober and direct.

"Thanks for taking the time with me," she said. "I must have been impossible."

"Impossible?" he echoed. "No. Anything but. That you're standing here is proof of that."

The Socrates Smith Notebook

<u>Conversation with Dr. Frederick Frolich:</u>
    A lesson in patience

Patience gives time for perspective.
Perspective leads to appreciation.

Appreciation is an antidote to the emptiness
that comes from too much of a good thing. Or the
emptiness that comes from fear that we don't have
enough.
Happiness rests on patience, the patience to let
life unfold, to recognize that the greatest joys may
come slowly or when we least expect them.

"Patience is the companion of wisdom."
    -St. Augustine

"Slow and steady wins the race."
    -Aesop

"Great works are performed not by strength but
by perseverance."
    -Samuel Johnson

"Patience is bitter but its fruit sweet."
   -Anonymous

"Diamonds are nothing more than chunks of coal that stuck to their jobs."
   -Malcolm Forbes

"Patience and tenacity of purpose are worth more than twice their weight of cleverness."
   -Thomas Henry Huxley

"Nothing will be achieved by attempting to interfere with the future before the time is ripe. Patience is needed."
   -I Ching

"If I have ever made any valuable discoveries, it has owed more to patient attention than to any other talent."
   -Sir Isaac Newton

"Time ripens all things; no man is born wise."
   -Miguel de Cervantes

"Maturity involves being honest and true to oneself, making decisions based on a conscious internal process, assuming responsibility for one's decisions, having healthy relationships with others and developing one's own true gifts. It involves thinking about one's environment and deciding what one will and won't accept."
     -Mary Pipher

"The world is full of magical things patiently waiting for our wits to grow sharper."
     -Bertrand Russell

"Most men pursue pleasure with such breathless haste that they hurry past it."
     -Soren Kierkegaard

"A handful of patience is worth more than a bushel of brains."
     -Dutch proverb

"You won't help shoots grow by pulling them higher."
   -Chinese proverb

"Where there is charity and wisdom, there is neither fear nor ignorance. Where there is patience and humility, there is neither anger nor vexation."
   -Saint Francis of Assisi

   The reality is that many of us lead large portions of our lives as if we are in a desperate chase. We are either anaesthetizing ourselves with television and food and shopping and alcohol, or we are working desperately for success, money, security, or love. We settle for repeated shots of pleasure, perhaps at the cost of the pleasure that lasts and lasts...Happiness.
   With regard to many pleasures - sex, alcohol, food, when we buy new clothing or a new car or a home - the resulting 'high' diminishes in its intensity or ability to please within minutes, hours, or days, maybe months or years. Often, the higher the high, the bigger charge we need the next time around to

satisfy our need for that variety of pleasure.

On the other hand, it's not so easy to figure out what will bring happiness. And the things that usually bring it take time and repeated attention. Still, the pursuit of pleasure lends us a clue. Some pleasures require that we invest our time and ourselves in them.

Hobbies, for instance. Or passionate interests in one's job, family, or favorite social cause. They may not provide quick satisfaction or intense sensation. But often the satisfaction we derive from them grows over time, resonates deeply within us as if we have become something bigger than what we were - more knowledgeable, more charitable, more aware, or more capable - as a result of our pursuit. Such pleasures take time to unfold. They require patience.

CHAPTER SEVEN

MINITAUER

B y the time I reached the DΣLPHI, it was after 9:00 AM. Sophie had taken an early break. George wore a bright florid tie with a chamois sport coat that looked like it had come off the flanks of a palomino pony.

"You're looking mighty dapper today, George," I said, catching a whiff of his cologne, a breezy Mediterranean scent.

He looked at me warily. George was suspicious of comments about his appearance, and had become downright nervous, I surmised, trying to decipher the word "dapper."

"Your tie. Your sport coat," I said, smiling. "You look wonderful, like a gentleman on his way to an important meeting."

His face broadened into a grin. He pulled a stack of 20-dollar bills from the cash register and counted them proudly.

"I meet with bank officers later today," he said. "To get loan. Soon George Niketopoulous will have big restaurant."

"That's wonderful, George," I said. "They couldn't put their money in better hands!"

"Maybe." He paused as doubt suddenly intruded. "Everything maybe."

"I believe in you, George," I said. "Your customers, your friends…they believe in you, too. Trust me."

Doubt passed as quickly as it had come. Hope flickered in his eyes again.

"Smith, I serve you best Greek meal you ever have when I open new restaurant," George said.

"Thanks, George. I'm already looking forward to it! I hope," I added, trying to reassure him, "that your meeting goes well."

"You hope?! I hope!" said George, his eyes bugging, huge and portentous.

I dropped a dollar and change on the counter, took my mug and the paper to a quiet booth in the back of the DƐLPHI.

None of the newspaper headlines could hold my interest. I thumbed through the Wednesday sports section until I reached the high school sports pages. Biff Rawlings' column focused on the upcoming gridiron match-up between our boys from Exley High School and neighboring Carter Academy. Much to my delight, a photo of young quarterback Eddie Smith accompanied the column. I read the news of my son proudly. Eddie was having a breakout season and was now capturing the attention of the local press. Carrie had heard that a local college scout might even be eyeing him. Because he was only a sophomore, I had my doubts and mostly just hoped Eddie would continue to play well and have fun.

I tore the page carefully from the paper for the family. Randy would ride his brother mercilessly for his sudden brush with renown. *Younger brother* was a humbling role. As I rose to leave, I bumped abruptly into a gruff-looking man in a trench coat.

"Pardon me," I said. Unable to catch my balance, I slipped back into my chair.

He did not reply. Hands in his pockets, pipe hanging loosely from his lips, he loomed over me like an oak tree's lamplight shadow.

"What do you want?" I asked. His menacing manner annoyed as much as perplexed me.

"What do I want?" he replied, straight-faced. He struck a match and touched it to the pipe bowl. His cheeks pumped like bellows until he had conjured a thick cloud of smoke. With quizzical gaze, he said: "Isn't the question, what do *you* want?"

And before I could muster a response, he was out the door.

Regaining my composure, I started to make my way to the front as Sophie returned from her break.

"You dropped something," she said, stooping over and grabbing a sealed envelope from the floor.

"Not mine," I said. "It might belong to that character in the trench coat."

"No," she said, examining the envelope and handing it to me. "I think this belongs to you."

There, written on the envelope in large, handsome script, was *SMITH*.

I tore it open. In the same heavy-handed script, it carried a cryptic message.

> *Bring the quest to the Quad*
> *Tonight at 7:30.*
> *Hope, this starts you off.*
>
> *PM*

"Do you know this guy?" I asked.

"Who?"

"The trench coat guy. Looks like a bulldog with a fedora," I said. "An odd guy. A moment ago, I thought he wanted to duke it out with me."

"Scared ya, huh?" she snickered.

"Surprised me," I said, holding back a grin. "I can hold my own."

"Good," she said. "No one likes going to the Quad at night." She shot an elbow into my ribs as she passed. "Except maybe you tough guys."

Then it was back to the job search. I called a number of business acquaintances and met with a good friend who had recently started his own small manufacturing company. Before I knew it, I was having lunch with Louie Franco, a former colleague who was laid off when I was. I was looking forward to hearing how he was doing.

Louie wore shadows of restlessness under his eyes. He looked like he had aged five years in the days since the axe had fallen.

"I'm too old for stuff like this," he moaned.

"Talent is never too old, Louie," I said. "There are hundreds of companies you could contribute to."

"Name one," he demanded. "Schaeffer? Workinetics? I've tried them already."

"Why limit yourself to the old competitors?" I asked. "Try thinking outside the box. Maybe look at a different industry altogether."

"You can't teach an old dog new tricks," he retorted.

The ping-pong of clichés was tiring, and, worse, would get us nowhere.

"You're not as bad off as you think. No one is," I added. "Opportunities will open up. Just see!"

"Smith, maybe I'm missing something, but I don't see companies lining up to make *you* their next CEO."

"I guess they don't know what they're missing."

"And they never will!" said Franco. "That's the problem. You spend your professional career going the extra yard. The company tells you how important you are. A loyal employee. But in the end, you're a cost item. Expendable. You wake up one morning to find that your work meant nothing. All I want is a well-defined job I'm suited for and a steady paycheck. I've got obligations and a lifestyle my wife and I are accustomed to. That's all I need," Louie continued. "That's not a lot to ask for, is it?"

"I wish I could help, Louie," I said. "If there's anything I can do…"

"Thanks, Smith. But forgive me if I don't hold my breath."

I decided it would do no good to suggest other career possibilities to Franco. He would hear none of my suggestions. As far as he was concerned, life had dealt him a blow below the belt. Forget fair play, loyalty, and just reward. Loyal Louie Franco had come to a grim, unoriginal conclusion: in the work world, it's every man for himself, and damn the naïve fool who expects his fair share of the pie from the powers that be.

I could tell I'd be wasting my time trying to convince him otherwise.

No encouraging words could parry his sense of certain defeat and cosmic injustice. I wished I could have shown him that the world was full of opportunities. But I could see that none of my messages had a chance of getting through. Besides, at the moment, I was speaking from a weak platform – at least in Louie's eyes.

My watch wasn't the only thing telling me it was time to go. Louie thanked me as I picked up the bill. By the time I hit the street, I felt like I had just awakened from a bad dream. I did my best to clear my head. Louie's sense of hopelessness had made me restless and uneasy. He had shut the door on any prospects other than the staid life to which he had grown accustomed. What a difference from the optimism of Stover and Frolich. I decided to put Louie out of my mind. Other matters begged for attention. I tried to recall the message from the note that had been left for me at the DΣLPHI: "Hope this starts you off." Something about that line bothered me. What was it?

As soon as I left the office, I pulled the message from my pocket again.

I read the line again: *Hope, this starts you off.*

A misplaced comma. Was that what was bothering me?

Carrie met me at the practice field. The Exley High School football team had separated for skill drills. Linemen worked on blocking the pass rush in a far corner of the field. The place kicker and his two-man entourage clubbed balls through the near uprights. But it seemed that everyone had at least one eye on the aerial show put on by the guys in the red pinnies.

With the playoffs approaching, Eddie was an untouchable on the practice field. A gold flap over the red net served as visible warning – "Hands off!" – to the burly linemen on the Exley squad. They all knew their ticket to a conference championship depended a lot on Eddie.

Eddie, agile and rawboned, took a long snap from the center and cupped the ball to his ear. His receiver broke from a set stance, dipped his shoulder inside. That was all the bait his defender needed. Gazelle-like, the red-clad receiver ate up ground. Eddie's arm cocked like a gun-hammer, and the oblong ball arced high into the air. Forty yards downfield, it settled neatly into the hands of the receiver at full stride. Whoops and handclaps followed.

My kid or not, Eddie was impressive. I would like to have stayed and watched longer, but I had follow-up calls to make. Word had begun to circulate that I was available. I might have lost my job, but I hadn't lost my reputation. I kissed Carrie and left for the library.

I spent the rest of the afternoon gathering information for my upcoming job interviews. After dinner with the family, I was off again. My destination this time was the grand spread of garden, concrete, and design that comprised the Quad.

The bronze statues rose high above the gate on the north end. I passed them, holding to the park's perimeter. I turned left and followed the vertical iron rails backed by dense hedge growth until I reached the opening to the maze.

By day, the maze is a pleasant place of fancy, as inviting a walk as one can take in our city. It's not everyone's delight at night, however. Now, even with well-spaced street lamps, the maze was full of nooks and shadows where a predator in waiting might surprise a passerby. No season passed without some of the local citizenry calling for more police protection in the vicinity of the Quad or even leveling the maze itself in the name of public safety.

But the protests never made headway, for the maze had become a part of city pride and identity. It bends and breaks through tall hedge growth with false openings and dead ends. At every turn, it provides surprise. Where the path finally narrows and seems lost in its own intricacy, a small opening appears, and the maze opens dramatically into the fountain square.

The mood shifted from peaceful to eerie as I entered the maze's interior. As many times as I had passed through it, I had become certain of one thing: a good maze mouse I would never be. Between the ever-changing labyrinth and my own memory lapses, I was good for a wrong turn or two, night or day.

Between turns, I thought about the guy in the trench coat and the message that I assumed he had dropped. The shadows and soughing of the wind through the hedge growth heightened my senses to any sign of the unusual. A wrong turn had me retracing my steps and embarking on a new route.

Finally, smelling the aroma of thick pipe tobacco smoke, I moved closer to the hedgerow and touched the leaves. Pinpoints of amber light broke through the foliage. I sidled along the hedgerow. A breath of smoke curled ghostlike in the faint light before me…the heavy cherry aroma of cured tobacco.

A muffled cough broke the silence.

"You're not sure, are you?" the voice asked. I found myself at the egress to the maze.

Dark shadows concealed his face. Smoke billowed from his pipe. His long coat fell in a rumpled pattern of shadow and light. The hot embers of tobacco flared, then faded into a dull glow. He made no move. I sensed no threat.

"Sure about what?" I answered, moving in an arc, stopping finally before him.

"What you are doing here."

"No," I said cautiously. I breathed more easily with my back to the fountain and the open Quad. Outside the tight corridors of the maze, the park had opened like a wide river. For the first time that evening, the moon poked its face through the clouds. The fountain babbled a steady tune that reminded me of a brook in the Catskills that I had visited often during my early teens.

"That's the nature of the search," he said, speaking as if he could peer into my thoughts. "It can seem vague, ephemeral…an unsettled state of the soul. Most people are lucky if they catch a fleeting glimpse of what they're after. Even then, they can't hold onto it long enough to figure out what it is." He sent another cloud of smoke into the silver light.

"And what is this search?" I asked. "What is this elusive thing I can't get a hold of?"

He arose from the bench and the shadows, and I recognized the taut facial lines, the thick brow and the dark eyes that had peered at me at the DΣLPHI that morning.

He looked at me smugly.

"Happiness, of course," he said.

Of course.

"Who are you?" I asked.

"Minitauer is the name," he said. "Paul Minitauer."

"Like the Minotaur," I said. "The bull-man of the labyrinth. How poetic."

He thrust his hands into his coat pockets. Pipe smoke hung around him like a swarm of bees.

"The note," I said. "Why did you ask me here?"

He just grunted. "Do you know what a labyrinth is? Most people think it's a maze, meant to confuse people for amusement and entertainment. But it is an ancient meditation tool that dates back thousands of years and actually was never originally intended to confuse the traveler at all but, instead, was designed as a well-marked path to provide direction. Walking the path provides quiet time for reflection. For a spiritual journey."

I had never heard that before and found that information interesting. "I wonder how many people know that," I replied. Minitauer's response was brief and to the point. "Let's go," he said.

And we were off.

Minitauer was light on his feet and moved quickly. I hustled to keep up with him.

"Happiness," he began after we had walked silently for two blocks. "Everyone wants it. Nearly everyone agrees that it is the most universal of human pursuits. But that's where agreement ends. What is happiness? What does the word mean? Try out a definition. Try to figure out what happiness means to you. Then ask the next guy."

Yes, I thought. If we all want it, why can't we agree on what we need to secure it and just *have* it? Is it the same for everyone? Do we all, deep down, want the same things?

We walked along the edge of the nightlife district, past storefronts and office buildings into the heart of the downtown business district. Two blocks further west, we entered a quiet block of old bungalows and apartment buildings that comprised the primary residential architecture of 80 or so years ago.

In the middle of the block, he stopped and held open the wrought iron gate that spanned sections of a chest-high brick wall. The walkway led to an enormous Victorian dwelling with turrets and a huge porch that wrapped around the south side of the house. The moonlight cast dark shadows across the driveway and gave the home an intriguing Gothic quality.

"You do have a flare for the dramatic," I said.

The massive oak door was at least ten feet high with a tall inset of thick, leaded glass. As we entered, amber light filled the foyer. I admired the carved mahogany bench, a beautiful antique bordered by two umbrella stands topped with carved seahorse heads. A red Persian rug straddled the stairway. Under other circumstances, I might have begged for a tour of the house. But that would have to wait.

Thick, sculpted balusters supported a handsome rail at the top of the stairs. There we entered a well-tended study lined with bookshelves that filled two entire walls. His desk was massive, and an enormous globe marked by nations of the ancient world dominated the far corner.

He kept his coat and hat on and slumped into the chair behind his desk.

"You have a beautiful home," I quipped, prompting no reply.

A lone volume lay open on a bookstand of red maple.

"What are you reading?" I asked.

"See for yourself."

It was Aristotle's *Nicomachean Ethics*, opened to the fourth chapter.

"The section on happiness?" I asked.

"I thought you might find the subject matter interesting."

It was handsome text with florid capital letters opening each chapter. Indecipherable notes were crowded in the margins.

"Refresh my memory," I said. "It's been about twenty years since I've looked at that!"

"This is the section in which Aristotle said that almost everyone, poor and rich, foolish and wise, would agree that happiness is the universal and highest goal of man. But what makes them happy? Ah. That's where they differ."

"Most people, according to Aristotle, think happiness is something simple and obvious. Like pleasure or fame. But these folks think that what they need to be happy is out of their reach or in too short a supply. They don't have enough money. Enough fame. Everyone thinks it is something different. In fact, the same person will likely change his tune in accordance with his condition. The poor man thinks wealth will bring happiness. Should he gain wealth but incur a physical ailment, suddenly health becomes the key to happiness. What they all have in common is fear. Fear driven by a scarcity mentality, even in a world of abundance!"

"Then there's pleasure," I interjected. "Some would simply equate happiness with a variety of pleasures, like a mixed box of chocolates."

"Yes," said Minitauer. "That's another view of happiness, as widespread today as ever. But how is that different from the life of a well-kept dog? Sleep. Eat. Have the master pet you whenever you want."

"I guess we all have times when that will do," I retorted, but drew no response from my companion. "Fame, honor, reputation," I said, returning to the prevailing views. "Many would regard the adulation of others as necessary for happiness."

"But, as the wise – and anyone wrongfully accused – know, you can't hang your happiness on what other folks think of you," responded Minitauer. "That leads some to look to virtue as the ticket to happiness."

"But can you equate virtue with happiness?" I asked. "I'll concede that virtue has its rewards, but I'm not convinced it's the main stuff of happiness."

Minitauer drew deeply from his pipe, and his mouth spread into an ironic grin. "Temperate with drink, chaste, well-mannered…Not even Aristotle could equate that kind of virtue with happiness," he chortled. "It's great to be able to handle life's insults and injuries, but that's not what we mean by happiness."

"But many of the things we are talking about are still part of the happy life," I interjected. I thought about my recent encounters. "I mean, we shouldn't dismiss them. In fact, I would say it's hard to be truly happy without virtue. And, to be honest, I don't know how happy one can be without some old-fashioned pleasure thrown in."

"Can't disagree with that," he said, tapping his pipe and admiring it.

He leaned across the desk. "Aristotle went on to make a critical point: that happiness, true happiness, goes beyond virtue, beyond a mere state of mind. People don't just think. They act. And the right kind of action will lead to pleasant results. And things like friends, money, power and even happiness may just be the by-product of leading a good life."

I was getting anxious to move beyond an academic discussion and focus more on something tangible. Something I could wrap my hands around and use today. "But," I wondered, "this material goes back two and a half millennia. How far have we come in all those years in understanding happiness? For all the interest in happiness, for all the time that minds like Aristotle and others have devoted to analyzing it, what do we have to show for it? Hasn't someone boiled it down to its component elements, for all to follow?"

"A formula, you mean?"

"Yes, I guess that's what I mean. In a way. I'm not here to rehash Aristotle but to discover a formula. The secret Code to Happiness. If there is such a thing."

"For a man who just learned patience, you seem awfully impatient," he chided. I started to ask what he meant by the remark, how he had learned about my conversation with Frolich on this subject, but he waved off my question.

"OK. Sorry," I said. "But I believe I'm onto something even though I don't know exactly what. But for all the talk tonight – every night lately, for that matter – I'm not sure how far I'm getting. Aristotle talks about *taking action* as a key to happiness. Well, isn't it time for me to take some action?"

Minitauer drew on his pipe. For more than a minute, the room was silent. Finally, he spoke. "All right," he said. He slid back his chair and opened the top drawer of his desk. He pulled out a hand-sized object. "Here," he said, extending it across the desk.

It was a broken piece of brass with braided design and dark lettering in relief. The last letter was broken. H-O-l, it read.

"What is this?" I asked.

"You'll have to find out for yourself. But I will say this. You're right. Action is part of the key to happiness. But most people not only don't know what to do, they don't know where to *start* when they finally figure out what they need to do. You want to take action? Great! This will help you know where to begin."

"What do you mean?" I asked.

He rose from his chair and circled the desk. "You have enough to get going," he said. "Good luck."

"Hey, I'm sorry. I didn't mean to break up the conversation," I said. Our dialogue had taken a wrong turn.

"That's all right, Smith," he said. "I'm getting tired, and you have enough to get going."

He led me to the door pondering his puzzling remark. The hallway was dimly lit. I reached for the doorknob and turned back to him.

"Where do I go from here?" I asked, pleading for more guidance.

I could barely make out his face in the shadows.

"Like I said," he replied matter of factly. "You have enough to get going."

I had plenty of time to think on the long walk back to the Quad. Stray headlamps and a few well-bundled people were the only signs of life on the street.

Over and over, I replayed our conversation in my mind. Happiness was the ultimate desire of everyone. But where were the answers? Was happiness something too slippery to get a noose around? Was it something tailored differently to every man and woman without threads of consistency? Some of the greatest minds had pondered happiness and left us their thoughts. And where had it gotten us? If happiness were something different for everyone, then are all of us on our own?

But, different as we all are, aren't we bound together in something called humanity? Certainly we must have enough in common so that those who'd searched for happiness throughout history offered clues or guidelines for others alive today.

What else had he said? "Happiness is about *action*." Did he mean that it was not merely a quiet state of bliss? Perhaps. For what a fragile gift happiness would be if it evaporated the second we departed our happy mental state and met the challenges of living in the real world.

Finally, I arrived at the maze entrance, a short distance from my car. It was nearly midnight. My automobile sat alone, its black finish bathed in lamplight. But some vague instinct tugged at me. I found myself walking back into the maze, drawn by an urge much stronger than the apprehension of the darkness and potential danger of the maze and its shadows.

Unlike earlier, I moved alert and faultless through the maze. I made no wrong turns into dead end passages, needed no reference points to find my way.

Before I knew it, I had passed through the opening. The fountain continued to babble. No other sign of life, not even a breath of wind, passed through the Quad.

I stood at the site where I had met Minitauer, then walked to the bench where I had first seen him.

My foot struck something small but solid. Lamplight glanced off its face. I picked it up.

It felt like a hefty paperweight. I turned it over and noticed its broken edge and the letter "E" in a familiar script.

I reached into my pocket for the piece of broken brass that Minitauer had given me only shortly before. One now in each hand, they felt strikingly similar. I fumbled with them, then matched the broken edges.

The fit was perfect. The letter "P" now apparent in the combination of the two pieces. The word they assembled was unmistakable.

I read it aloud.

> ## *"HOPE"*

The Socrates Smith Notebook

Conversation with Paul Minitauer:
A lesson in hope...

"I am not discouraged because every wrong
attempt discarded is another step forward."
-Thomas Edison

"Every area of trouble gives out a ray of hope;
and the one unchangeable certainty is that nothing
is certain or unchangeable."
-John Fitzgerald Kennedy

"Hope is the best possession. None are
completely wretched but those who are without
hope, and few reduced so low as that."
-William Hazlitt

"In all pleasure, hope is a considerable part."
-Samuel Johnson

"Strong hope is a much greater stimulant to life than any single realized joy could be."
-Friedrich Nietzsche

"Your hopes, dreams and aspirations are legitimate. They are trying to take you airborne, above the clouds, above the storms, if you only let them.
-William James

"Hope tells us tomorrow will be better."
-Tibullus

"My hopes are not always realized, but I always hope."
-Ovid

"He who has health, has hope; and he who has hope has everything."
-Arabian proverb

"Hope: A species of happiness, and perhaps the chief happiness which this world affords."
-Samuel Johnson

"To travel hopefully is a better thing than to arrive."
-Robert Louis Stevenson

CHAPTER EIGHT

MONEY TALK

Bippita, bippita, bippita, bippita, boomp/clunk...

The gourd-shaped leather bag marked "Everlast" spun from its swivel, shuddered a brief paroxysm, then rocked faintly.

My shoulders clicked in their sockets. Nodules and knots and whatever other insults lactic acid brings to the muscles flared in protest beneath my skin. I felt like a bag of creaking joints, and, for the moment at least, like the poster boy for all out-of-shape middle-aged men of America.

It was only temporary, I reminded myself, mesmerized by the faintly swinging bag. I couldn't be in as bad shape as I felt. It had only been a couple of weeks since I had exercised, not the months of neglect my muscles and bones seemed to claim.

Bippita, bippita, bippita. I had better rhythm now. Shoulders not so tight. Build up speed more slowly this time. Bippita, bippita, bippita. There you go. I had mounted the speed bag to the wall. Whoppita, whoppita, whoppita. Deep thwacking sounds said my punch *was* coming back.

My fist landed deep into the leather with each clout, hands picking up speed with every touch. A minute passed. Yes, it was coming back. Shoulders still a little tight, yes. Hands a little heavy. Push through the fatigue.

A hot flame flashed from my fist.

I examined the half-inch flap of skin. The leather ring around the bag's valve had nearly sheared off the top of my middle knuckle. Damn. Should have worn the gloves. Where were those things anyway? And there they were, right in front of me, wedged at the base of the 2 by 4 buttress. Right where I had left them. In August, of course.

I nudged the flap of skin back over the knuckle, and it burned more. Can't quit this soon, I told myself. It was bad enough I had neglected exercise. Didn't need a setback. Now I'd added ground-meat knuckles to yesterday's sore muscles. Bad start only two days into the new and improved Kid Smitty's health regimen. I had run a hard mile the day before and added sets of push-ups, squat jumps, and a few sets with the dumbbells. It hadn't been the toughest workout, but my body was arguing otherwise.

The glove felt coarse. It chafed against the open knuckle. I pounded the bag with the bottom of my right fist. The hands lacked grace now, but they were on the money. After a few minutes of pounding, I felt I had done my time, tested my mettle enough for Day Two of my "get-in-shape" comeback. When I removed the gloves, beads of blood had replaced the raw orange pulp beneath the knuckle flap.

The neighborhood cat had wandered into the yard – no doubt to watch me train. "Winner and still block champion, Socrates Smith!" I announced to my feline fan, shaking a fearsome fist to make my point. Yep. That name would send waves of fear through the heavyweight ranks.

"What was that name?" asked Randy.

I looked up. Randy was nodding like a bobble head doll. His smirk reminded me of Allen Funt after one of his old Candid Camera stunts.

"Nothing. Just muttering to myself."

"Still pretty quick for an old dude."

I scanned the garage. "Who's that? Did somebody old just come in here?"

"Sorry," he said. A corner of his mouth curled. "What'd you do, put your hand in a meat grinder?" He cocked his head for a better view of the fist. "So this is what happened to the bare-knuckles champions. No wonder they switched to gloves."

"Timing's off. Just trying to get back in shape. It gets a little tougher each time you lay off."

Randy grew suddenly quiet.

"I need to talk to you, Dad," he said. "Do you have a minute?"

"Sure. The great comeback can wait five minutes. What's up?"

"It's about that recording offer."

"Yeah? I've been meaning to talk with you. I wasn't exactly sure what happened at breakfast the other day. Or that I liked the way we left that conversation."

"Yeah. Sorry about that."

"I'm sorry, too. Fill me in on the details."

Randy had bounced from band to band for years without much luck. Then came Man on the Run. He had brought this band together, and it bore his signature all the way. He had poured all manner of energy into the band. He had even served as the group's manager, booking all the early gigs.

A lot of the music was pure noise to my aging musical sensibilities. Still, I had to admit that the songs he had written gave the group a unique, energetic sound. Over the course of time and countless practice sessions, Randy tweaked the numbers with fresh harmonies. Now, lo and behold, Man on the Run had become one of the hottest groups in the city.

The recording contract at issue would not only be the consummation of Randy's dream, it would also be his validation: for his talent and for his persistent pursuit of his dream. I thought about "patience" and realized how patient Randy had been over the years. He had stuck with his dream and his music through drummers without rhythm and guitarists with the stage energy of a rock. He had hung tough against my parental caveats and expressions of concern. I was sure that he had an "I-told-you-so" speech already prepared for me if his fortunes made the turnabout that he was now expecting.

When Randy was in high school, we had run the gamut of discourse on the subject, from reasonable discussions to high-pitched argument. But he had decided upon a career in music in early adolescence, and he had focused on his dream like a laser beam. For the last two years, we had held to an unspoken truce on the subject. Gradually my skepticism had yielded to tolerance. He was still looking for my support and encouragement. That he had found me now to discuss his dilemma helped me to clear most of the regrets from our earlier encounters out of my cluttered brain. Do the right thing, Smith, I reminded myself. Criticizing your son or embarrassing him won't be much help. If he's gung-ho about becoming a musician, maybe he could use your help. After all, this is his passion.

As much as Randy wanted this recording contract, his instincts had been whispering warnings. An independent recording company, Blue Records, Inc., had approached him with an unconventional contract. The contract was heavily back-loaded. Randy would receive no money up front and none until the company's initial investment in Man on the Run recordings – so far, unspecified – had been covered. Only then would the band get a piece of the action. Furthermore, the company wanted Randy to enter into a second contract, independent of the group, guaranteeing them the recording rights to any subsequent songs he wrote.

"I know this seems like a dream come true, Randy, but the contract seems awfully one-sided," I said. "You better check these guys out, talk things over with an attorney who understands this field. It doesn't sound like you have any guarantee that they'll market your songs aggressively. You could be signing yourself into a black hole."

Randy looked up slowly. Disappointment more than anger showed in his eyes.

"They said that we'd be getting the bulk of their attention, that they'd hit all the local record stores and work with radio stations across the country." His voice exposed his doubts.

"Maybe they will. It could be a great deal," I said. "But follow up with the attorney."

"I don't have much money. I've got a little saved for some new equipment. That's about all," he said.

"I'll cover the first appointment for you."

"Are you sure, Dad?"

"Yep, I'm sure. I want to help you, Randy. Just give me fair warning when you find the right attorney. Let me know the damages."

"Thanks, Dad. Thanks a lot."

I mopped the beads of sweat from my forehead with my sleeve. A chill had set in while I was talking to Randy. My will to run began to waver, so I touched my toes and lunged and twisted and took to the pavement before I could talk myself out of the roadwork. My legs felt tight as I tried to build some momentum. One foot in front of the other. Ignore the discomfort. Before long, my stride would smooth out, and the pace would become less labored. Couldn't be soon enough.

By the time I had returned to our driveway, I had added another quarter mile to yesterday's distance. My lungs were still working hard, and breath came in hot gulps. But I was feeling better, confident I was back on track.

Eddie exploded out the front door as if he were shedding a tackler. The door slammed, and he bounded down the stairs.

"I wondered where you were," he said.

"Just logging some miles," I said, hands on my knees. "Well, one and a fraction at least."

"Excited for the game on Saturday?"

"Can't wait. Why do you ask?

"Oh, no reason, really," he said. "It's just that you've been pretty busy lately. I was just wondering…is everything OK?"

"Yeah, Eddie. I'm OK," I said. "Great, in fact."

"New job?"

"Not yet," I said. Eddie bit his lip slightly. "It's coming, though. Things are coming along. Better than I could have hoped for."

"Yeah?"

"Sure are!" I said, believing it, too.

The carpool kids waved a greeting as Eddie boarded the mini-van. Two of the others were football players. They were loud and just rowdy enough to convince me they were ready to play Carter on Saturday. I waved and watched them disappear around the corner.

At least they knew their destination.

Carrie was in the kitchen, paying bills. I hugged her, kissed her forehead.

"You're a sweaty guy," she said.

"That's hard-earned sweat," I countered.

"Speaking of hard-earned…"

I cut her off before she could finish. "Please. Don't worry about the finances," I said.

Carrie looked at me and frowned.

"That's not all I'm worried about," she said. "It seems like you have a lot of nighttime appointments these days. Dinner interviews. Evening meetings. I'm starting to worry. It seems like every day you have another meeting, but I never hear much about the jobs you're going after."

"There's not much to say."

"There must be *something* to say. I rarely hear anything about the company, about the job. Your description of the people you've been out with is always vague, mysterious."

"Yeah. Well, they are kind of mysterious."

Her look oscillated between anger and pain. "Please. Sarcasm isn't going to help."

"I'm not being sarcastic."

"Then what's going on?"

"They're not all about jobs…at least, not directly." I felt like I was stumbling.

She sat quietly. "What are you looking for?" she asked. She was perturbed, confused.

"Happiness," I said, hoping I hadn't opened Pandora's box.

"Happiness?" she replied, looking at me with bewilderment and concern.

I knew my answer sounded strange. How could I expect her to understand – or believe – in a quest for a Code to Happiness?

"Honestly, dear. I'm focusing on happiness. There's nothing going on that you need to worry about. These people: Stover. Rube. This other fellow, Minitauer. They're all part of something I don't completely understand, but it's tied into happiness. My happiness. Our happiness. Everyone's happiness, in a way."

"And this woman? Ellen mentioned you had a strange conversation with a waitress at the DƩLPHI?"

"Yes, Sophie – the waitress at the DƩLPHI Café – she's part of it, too. But, trust me, there is nothing to worry about."

She sat in tight-lipped silence. Her face was a four-layered cake with puzzled eyes atop flaring nostrils, a loving mouth, and a stubborn jaw unwilling to buy into anyone's nonsense, including mine.

"I'm not hiding anything. Only trying to make sense of some very strange conversations. I can try to explain it to you. But, honestly, I don't think it would make much sense right now."

The silent kitchen seemed filled with ears. Even the refrigerator magnets seemed anxious for answers I could not give them.

"We're all searching for happiness, Mr. Smith," Carrie said finally.

"Believe me, this search is different!" I said.

"Just be careful where you look. And how hard you look."

"Trust me," I said. "You know you can."

Then she added: "Ever hear of something called 'obsession'?"

"Can a quest become an obsession?" I asked.

"I don't know," said Carrie. "But I don't think obsession and happiness make for a good mix."

"I love you," I said.

"I love you, too," she said with a smile I treasured in that moment as much as I would treasure any face of happiness. "I do love you."

The phone rang.

"I wonder what this ring will bring?" said Carrie. She grabbed the phone and pointed it toward me, handing over the receiver. "Here. You take it...it might be one of your 'happy' friends."

"Smith? This is Philip Stover."

"Philip. Hello."

Carrie mouthed "Stover?" I nodded.

She seemed pleased.

"I have a proposal for you," said Stover.

"A proposal?" I said. Carrie shook her small fist in triumph. "What kind?"

"I'd rather pitch you in person. Can you come down to my office?"

"Sure. Say when."

"How about eleven o'clock?"

"I'll be there. Anything I should bring?" I asked.

"Just your brain. You won't even need your charm and wit."

"Good," I said, glancing at Carrie. "I just lost those a few minutes ago."

"Fine. I'll see you at eleven."

Carrie gave me an extra long "I-don't-get-you-but-I-love-you" hug at the door. Silently, I thanked Stover.

His timing couldn't have been better. His reputation for making things happen left me intrigued. I was excited, thinking about a potential job opportunity.

I checked in with the receptionist fifteen minutes early, expecting to cool my heels until eleven. But Josephine came out almost instantly to lead me to his office.

"Mr. Stover is anxious to see you," she said.

"Well, thank you. I'm looking forward to seeing him as well," I said.

He was engaged in conversation when I arrived. Afraid I had entered at an awkward moment, I motioned toward the door. He shook his head vigorously and motioned for me to sit down.

"I understand," he said into the receiver. "Yes. I know. Eight million is eight million. I'd rather face the facts with our people now. There may be some opportunities to work through the current situation. No...I'll send a letter out to the shareholders explaining these developments...Sure. I realize that...But I'm looking into a strategic shift in direction that might help us make it back and then some within a year. Besides, without the trained workforce at that plant, we won't be able to take advantage of the opportunities when the economy turns. We just have to move swiftly on the adjustments...That's right...I think that will work...Great idea....OK. Let's talk again tomorrow."

He hung up and stretched a hand across the table. His handshake was firm.

"Glad you could make it on such short notice," he said. "Sorry for the delay. Some business needed attention."

"It's good to see you again. I enjoyed our conversation the other day. In fact, I've given it a lot of thought."

"I did, too. I've done some checking on you, Smith. It appears you have developed quite a reputation as a business analyst and strategic planner. If you're interested, we could use your help."

"What do you have in mind?" I asked.

Stover wasted no time in responding. "Let me fill you in. We acquired a company last year that we believed – believe – could help us better compete in the industrial controls market. We kept most of the management team. Talented folks. We thought we would give them a shot at righting the ship. Offered assistance where they needed it. I asked them to adopt a new workforce initiative that would empower workers down to the line level. But suddenly, panic set in. Key members of the management team bailed on us. I guess they thought we were setting them up for the slaughter when we had them meet with our other executives and introduced the new workforce concept. Nothing could have been further from the truth.

"But now my financial team and executive group are in a lather. They know we won't meet our projections for the year – not without a 'deus ex machina,' at least." He looked at me, testing my comprehension.

"'God from a machine.' The miraculous rescue in classic Greek drama."

"Good, Smith," he laughed. "My team," he continued, "is projecting a serious loss unless we make some major changes immediately. I have to trust their numbers."

"I understand," I replied.

"There's an easy answer that could prevent a significant loss of as much as eight million dollars. That's the conversation I was finishing up when you arrived. We could layoff staff, cut back the training program, trim operating costs to the nub," he said. He paused. "But we won't."

I listened quietly as Stover continued. "Actually, losses could be as high as ten million. Worst case scenario."

"That's a big number for any business."

Stover nodded in agreement and continued talking. "But, in my opinion, we would be throwing the baby out with the bath water if we pull the plug on this operation now."

He looked at me, trying to gauge my reaction. "We are committed to this program. It took us awhile to get the workers aboard, to get their commitment. Now that we have it, we owe it to them to follow through on our plan. We may not make our original projections, but we will rebound. If we resolve this situation, maybe we'll recover from these losses well before this time next year. I believe we can do that. And if we follow through and turn things around, which we *will* do, we will have built trust, and loyalty, too."

"And what is your plan, Philip?" I asked. "How can I help you?"

"We're getting ready to offer some early retirement packages, tighten up expenses in a couple of departments. As I said, the management team bailed on us. I'd like to retain your services to work on our team building. Help us put our people back together. We'll pay you at the same rate we pay our other consultants. You interested?"

Work. Even the word sounded good. Better still, I couldn't think of a more interesting person to work for.

We shook hands. "Count me in," I said.

As I sat in the office of one of our city's wealthiest businessmen, I began thinking about a topic that had me puzzled as I sought the key to happiness.

Money. It was a subject I wanted – and needed – to discuss.

Money factored, for better or for worse, into everyone's condition at one point or another. While I didn't believe money was the answer to all of my problems, or anyone else's, for that matter, I still couldn't ignore the opportunities money, particularly a lot of money, afforded.

At the same time, I had seen relatives fight over inheritance; business associates bite and bicker and jockey for high-paying promotions; families dissolve over money-driven ambition and uncontrollable spending habits. The root of all evil? Maybe not. But it caused enough mayhem to make you consider the proposition.

Besides, the subject had a stark immediacy for me on several fronts. I had been particularly sensitive to my personal financial situation since losing my job. I was about to engage in a team building exercise with management level employees who were concerned about their jobs and compensation. Perhaps more than anything, I realized I was sitting in the office of a man who could afford to lose millions of dollars in a business investment and be just fine.

I thought I'd raise the subject with Stover and get his take on money and happiness.

"Philip," I began. "You have a reputation for attracting money. You also seem happy. I'm wondering, what role do you think money plays in happiness?"

I wouldn't have been surprised if he had brushed the question aside or even deflected it with humor or sarcasm. He didn't.

"Fair question," he said. "The age-old underlying question is 'Can money buy happiness?' Right? The answer, of course, is 'No.' But, if I'm any judge of character, a one-word negative is not apt to satisfy you."

I just smiled back in silent response.

Philip rested his elbows on his desk chair, brushed his chin with his cupped fingers.

"Even those who know the answer wrestle with it," he went on. "I mean, an individual can totally believe and even preach that money does not buy happiness but still be thinking, 'Yeah, but happiness would still be a lot closer if I had a little more money, or maybe won the state lottery!' And to the extent that money meets needs and opens up possibilities, it can even be true. But what most people really want to know – and perhaps this is what you are asking – is, 'Would I be happier if the only question I had to answer were, 'What should I do with my money?' rather than 'Will I have enough?'

"Sigmund Freud sniffed out the facts early on in his practice," he went on. "He once said that he preferred working with wealthier patients. Know why? They already know that money can't buy happiness!"

"And, of course," I observed, "if it can't buy happiness, at least it affords the opportunity to choose one's own special brand of misery, right?"

Stover chuckled and continued. "I frequently meet with the owners of small to mid-sized companies. I know them well. Know their families, too. Many of them are wealthy people. A lot of these people, maybe most, aren't happy at all. In fact, a lot are downright miserable. They are afraid. They distrust everyone, often even those they love. Most of these people have lost their moral compass and suffer from greed. Their families come apart at the seams. Their children suffer from 'affluenza,' the disease of overindulgence and insufficient appreciation. Children learn to fight over who will get what or why one sibling appears to be getting more than another." He paused in the middle of his litany. "It goes on and on," he finished.

"But, clearly, it doesn't have to be that way," I observed. "People like you have used their money to expand opportunities. To pursue productive goals. To pursue your passions!"

Stover agreed. "The truth is that there's nothing wrong with money, but it is better to have passion! The happiest people I know have a lot more of that than money. It's the same thing in business. When passion drives a business, money flows in and out in a natural stream. The business, the dream, pouring energy into that dream and bringing that dream to life…money is only the *energy* that brings the dream to life. It's a different story when money becomes the focus!"

"Most people who start a business have passion. But can they sustain that passion, infect others with passion, too?" asked Philip. "Will successors or family members have that same love and passion for the business?

"All too often, the answer is 'No.' The labor of love – and sweat – that gave birth to the business turns into a struggle for control, control of the money the business generates. Many wealthy families end up fighting about money and losing focus on their business. That's no way to compete in a competitive world. Pretty soon, a nice family business is out of business or sold for a song," said Philip. "And a great family is torn apart at the seams."

I nodded my head. "Rags to riches to rags in three generations."

What is it about money, I had often wondered, that makes so many incredible ventures possible yet can make human beings so damned ugly and foolish that they are an embarrassment to the human race?

Stover recalled the oft-repeated observation that "money is the root of all evil."

"When you see a family fight over money or someone murdered during a robbery, you are apt to accept that principle," I said. "But when you need it to pay the rent or the grocery bill, you wish you had a little more of it. My guess would be that the more typical belief is that money is the root of all evil – for the other guy. Not for me."

"Let's take a closer look at that quote: 'Money is the root of all evil'," Stover replied. "Actually, historians believe that the quote originally came to us from St. Paul in his first letter to his disciple, St. Timothy. In his letter, he actually wrote that 'The *love* of money is the root of all evil.' Even though early Christians argued extensively over how man ought to regard wealth and possessions, Paul was careful to say that it's the *love* of money, not money itself, which is the root of all evil. But let's go on…If you're taking inventory of popular aphorisms about money, some of them would center on its importance."

"Sure," I blurted. "We have plenty of those. 'Money makes the world go 'round'."

"Exactly. And when you look at global problems that center on poverty – starvation, education, health care – to name just a few – the case might seem easily made. Even in affluent nations, we hear repeatedly that money is the leading source of marital problems and the leading cause of stress."

He pulled out a fresh dollar bill and wrote across one side in bold capital letters:

ROOT OF ALL EVIL

Then he flipped it over and wrote across the forehead of Washington:

KEEPS WORLD SPINNING

"So here are the two sides of money." He held the bill face up like a billboard, then flipped to its backside. He handed the bill to me. I noticed beside the penned word "EVIL" the tiny eye positioned at the top of the pyramid on the back of the bill. He turned the bill sideways, exposing only its thin paper edge.

"The truth about money is right here," he said. "How you walk this edge makes all the difference in the world."

He flipped the bill to its backside and pointed to it with the tip of his pen.

He set the bill down and, after a few quick strokes of his pen, cupped it in his hand.

"Ever stop to think about what money is?" he asked.

"I'll trust the dictionary," I said. "Something along the lines of 'a medium of exchange…with either a perceived or measurable value.' Yeah, something like that, I guess."

He handed the bill back to me. The word "EVIL" had disappeared. In its place read:

ENERGY

"This is how I prefer to think of it. I once heard money described as 'congealed' energy. Frozen or compressed energy awaiting some action by man to unleash its potential. It's neither bad nor good. It's just possibility for action. It's possibility for change. What kind of action it generates is purely up to us."

Stover paused in silent reflection before continuing. "How we use money, and how we think of money, is up to us. And that is a big part of what drives our happiness. That's about as much as I know."

I realized that was enough.

◇◇◇◇

Philip Stover rolled down the sleeves of his pinstripe shirt and fastened them at the wrist. Then he secured the button above his burgundy tie and tugged it snug.

"Enough money talk," he said. "Now. About your project…"

"Like Spock said, 'I'm all ears.'"

He walked around the desk and picked up the copy of an internal business report from one of the group leaders. As he flipped through its contents, I noticed again his thick fingers and the coarse hair that covered the back of his hands. He looked like he could still wield a shovel with his father and brothers. "This report holds quite a store of information," he said. "I'd like you to help me dig into it. Perhaps use it as a starting point to develop a plan to bring our team back together."

I scanned the report quickly. It was filled with financial statements and analysis. I put the report down and looked at Stover. "Let's get started!"

"I'm not anxious to lose eight million dollars," he said beneath a grin.

"I'll try not to disappoint you," I said, grinning back.

The Socrates Smith Notebook

Another conversation with Phillip Stover:
A lesson on money.

To sum up my conversation with Stover - money is neither good nor bad, assuming you have enough to take care of life's essentials. After that, money is what you make of it. It can be good or bad. It just depends on whether you use it intelligently to pursue passions, productive goals, and to help others in need or whether it's used to fuel greed, arrogance, and negative purposes.

I'm reminded of one of my favorite quotes...Rose Kennedy once said that "To whom much is given, much is required."

"Money doesn't always bring happiness. People with ten million dollars are no happier than people with nine million dollars."
   -Hobart Brown

"It is neither wealth nor splendor, but tranquility and occupation, which gives happiness."
   -Thomas Jefferson

"Try not to be a man of success, but rather try to become a man of value."
   -Albert Einstein

CHAPTER NINE

THE GAME

The game seemed to have a purpose independent of points and boundaries. The field blossomed with the bright hues of jerseys and helmets like tight bulbs on the brink of flower. Blends of red and yellow, white and blue exploded into motion, hovered in space, regrouped into communities of color only to break and burst again into more motion.

Eddie removed his helmet and motioned to me on the sideline. I nodded. In the next instant, my legs were light and fluid, gliding with long antelope-like strides, the earth barely a tickle to my foot at the bottom of each stride. The oblong ball was there when I turned, arriving neatly over my shoulder, settling softly in my hands.

The coach stood in the end zone, his wisdom stuffed in the pockets of his trench coat. His words were incomprehensible, and, as I turned my head to hear him, his coat had become a white robe.

Like a fortuneteller deciphering the etched network of a palm, I tried to read the lines of his face. A fringe of white hair now accented the smooth pate of Socrates. His laughter came as a deep rumble of joy that spread like an earth tremor. I awoke and noticed my bedroom was still. Rising up on my elbows, I waited for an echo or aftershock or other remnant from my quickly vanishing dream. All I could hear, however, was the hum of the alarm clock and the sounds of a far-off semi shifting gears on the open road.

My desk overflowed with loose ends. Everything lay where I had left it in the wee hours of the morning. I spent a few minutes organizing my notebooks into several neat stacks. When I was done, I surveyed the material that lay in front of me.

White sheets with punch-holes carried detailed notes and references to worker attitudes, performance reviews, awareness of company values and mission, and a dozen other matters relating to my project with Stover. Beneath them lay the report I had brought back from my meeting with him. Another notebook had its own special place on my desk. *The Socrates Smith Notebook*, it read in letters penned with a calligrapher's flourish. Loose pages held skeletal notes from my meetings with the likes of Ortiz and Stover. Memories of the meetings and stories and lessons of recent days and weeks flooded my mind. And atop them all lay something else.

HOPE

The broken fragments of metalwork I had been given and found two nights ago. What was this tarnished, broken relic? It looked like the remnants of some amulet or charm. Where had it come from?

The larger of the halves – the piece that Minitauer had handed me in his office – had a round eyelet at its top that hinted that it was worn to ward off evil or to bring its wearer happiness and good fortune. The piece that I had picked up in the Quad was the more sullied of the two. It was tarnished and caked with dirt, but the belly of the P and the letter E remained clear.

"Hope," I read aloud again. It was an intriguing charm. What was its origin? More importantly, what did it mean?

I forced my attention back to the report. Stover's project was welcome. It was a short-term project to determine the mind-set of the workers in the Sheffield plant following the exit of the former management team, and, based on that information, to help design a team building program to reestablish trust in the workplace. As I might have suspected, Stover wanted to peer beneath the surface of questionnaire responses that were currently being tabulated. For Phase One of the project, he expected a candid appraisal of worker attitudes. His commitment to his workforce was without question, but he was also determined to know exactly what he was up against.

Among my most important aims was determining how well the employees understood the situation. How deeply had the workers internalized the lofty company values and mission? Was it something they believed in? Did they realize that their jobs and their livelihood remained imperiled if the team could not rise to the occasion and commit to these values and mission? If not, Philip's new initiatives would only delay the inevitable.

My interest and sense of urgency in the project was soon comparable to any other project I had undertaken. I was working long hours to complete it well and on time. During break points in the course of each day, however, I found my mind turning over the substance of my conversations from the DΣLPHI Café. Trying to pull the pieces together and unlock, if there was one, the Code to Happiness.

"What's up, Dad?"

Eddie peered at me from the door of the library.

"You're up awfully early, Eddie," I said. "Pre-game excitement?"

"I just heard you rustling papers," he said.

"I don't know that you've ever looked better prepared than you did during this week of practice," I encouraged. "Just go out and play your game."

"Thanks, Dad," he said, plopping into the chair beside my desk. It wasn't often that he cornered me in my office. Eddie was not one to seek out support. Either he had the solitary, unflappable confidence of a gunfighter, or he was simply indifferent to praise. As his prowess on the gridiron demonstrated, Eddie had pockets of unmistakable talent. But he could also be remarkably blasé about areas that Carrie and I put stock in, particularly his education. He shined in subjects he took a liking to, but to our chagrin, seemed barely able to get through those classes he thought "b-b-b-borrring." I hoped he would catch on soon…

But today was no day for doubts of any kind.

"What's this Socrates Smith Notebook stuff?" he asked, sliding the loose notebook pages half hidden by the report for a better view.

"Just a few thoughts that have come to me that I wanted to keep track of," I answered. "In fact, maybe I'll come down to the locker room and give a little pep talk to your team!"

"Thanks, Dad. That would be great," Eddie said without trying to mask his sarcasm.

◇◇◇◇

I followed the wet footprints and the fresh fragrance of soap and deodorant from the bathroom into the kitchen. Eddie wore a white towel around his waist and a second draped over his shoulder. His finger lingered on the Post-it note stuck to the phone caddie. His voice broke before I could protest his wet feet.

"Room 228, Grandp, uh, Abraham Smith, please," he said into the remote.

Their conversation touched lightly on Dad's condition. Judging from the long stretches of quiet broken by the occasional "uh-hmm" and "I will," I figured Eddie was getting the usual earful of encouragement and advice from the "Grey Ghost," the nickname Dad had given himself to slip in earnest counsel on the greased skid of humor. "Take it from the Gray Ghost…," he would say. In spite of his humor, my father's words always had credibility with Eddie.

"How's he doing?" I asked when he had hung up. My presence surprised Eddie.

"Oh, he sounds great. I mean, his voice is kinda soft. But he's doing OK…I wish he could come to the game today…" Eddie's voice trailed into silence.

My heart sank like a U-boat in the Atlantic. "He'll catch the game on cable at the hospital. He'll be there in spirit."

"Yeah, sure," he said, dejected. His flat feet sounded like suction cups as he left the kitchen.

◇◇◇◇

The phone rang off the hook through breakfast as Ellen, now back at college, and several friends in town called to wish Eddie luck.

Carrie started breakfast. Eddie claimed he wasn't that hungry but then proceeded to scarf down three scrambled eggs, two large slices of ham, a bowl of cereal, and juice.

"Hey, big shot," roared Randy, slapping a bear hug on his brother. "'The kid with the golden arm.' How much did you have to pay Rawlings to say that in his column?"

"It was cheap. I just told him my big brother would wash his car every week for two months," said Eddie, blushing as he broke the hold.

"Bad bargain," Randy said. "Looks like I'll have to steal your allowance again." He punched Eddie in the arm.

Eddie flashed a backhand that caught Randy squarely on the shoulder. "Watch out, or I'll knot your hair to your headboard tonight, Big Brother."

"Enough already!" cried Carrie above our laughter.

"Thank God," I thought. "The kid is ready."

I called Dad. Eddie was right on one count. Dad's voice had lost even more of its resonance since I had spoken to him the day before.

The television played in the background. Anticipating a successful season and a strong local following after the team had flexed its muscles with impressive wins in the first two games, a local cable station had televised every Exley football game since, and Dad had switched it on early in anticipation.

"How are you doing, Dad?" I asked.

"Great," he replied, his voice cracking as he tried to add conviction. "How's Eddie? Butterflies?"

"None that I could see. Just excited," I said.

"I told him I got the best seat in the house," he said. "I'll have nurses bringing me food. I won't even have to stand in the hot dog line!"

"Enjoy the game, Dad. I'll try to stop by and say hello afterwards."

I hung up the phone and looked through the window. I could see Carrie starting up the car in order to drop Eddie off at the stadium.

The unfinished work in the library seemed to beg for attention. In the middle of the stacks of notebooks and texts, *HOPE* continued to glare at me from atop the pile on my desk. I couldn't get it off my mind. Was it a charm? A lesson? The more I tried to look past it to the matters that lay beneath, the more boldly it beckoned.

I picked up the right half and rubbed at the crusted dirt with my thumbnail. Powder and tiny chunks of compressed matter fell to the notebook. Minutes later, pressure and persistence had exposed an arc on the outer edge.

It looked as if equally diligent hands – those of Minitauer, I presumed – had rubbed the grime from the other half already.

I rested the piece against its companion once again and was amazed at the difference my minor attention had rendered. Parts of the charm now had faint luster. My hand scrubbing had extracted some hint of its former brilliance. I could see hair-thin veins of copper sheen and the dull aqua tint of patina. I had partially exposed tiny bits of detail – what looked like a braided border and ribbon-like flourishes.

A sudden thought had me rushing to the first floor linen closet. One shelf held scores of bottles bearing Carrie's nail polish, shoe sprays, and an assortment of specialty cleaners. I fumbled through a half dozen or more before I found it – a jar of jewelry cleaner I had seen her employ on rare occasions.

"Yes!" I grunted as I grabbed a handful of cleaning rags from a plastic bag.

Back in the study, I lifted a dab of cleaner with the cloth and applied it to the eyelet section of the amulet. I let it settle in for a good minute and then began to polish the face vigorously. When I wiped it clean, the eyelet and a section of gold braid sparkled like a hubcap on a prized antique automobile.

Twice more I applied the cleaner, and twice more nickel-size sections came gloriously alive beneath my cloth. I coated the left border with a dollop of cleaner and rubbed again. From out of the tarnish emerged the outline of a closed hand, index finger extended and slightly curved.

The rag was dark with dirt and tarnish. I rubbed it gently across the face of amulet, felt some of the dirt break beneath my fingers. My finger touched a small protuberance, smooth and hard. When I removed the cloth, a pair of surprises awaited me.

A ruby a quarter-inch across and a stone of yellow topaz.

My rush downtown was cutting it close. The game was only an hour and a half from kickoff. I had wedged the car into a No Parking zone in front of the DƐLPHI, leaving my left headlamp poking slightly into the traffic lane. Several of the café's patrons gave me an odd look as I muscled my way through them.

I held the pieces of the amulet in front of Sophie's nose, and she backed off reflexively like a far-sighted librarian.

"Look," I said. "What is this brass thing?"

Her eyes shuffled between my face and the objects in my hands.

"It's bronze, genius," she said, pushing a cup of coffee from a red-banded urn as gracelessly into my face as I had forced my discovery upon her. "Here try this," she added. "It looks like you need decaf this morning. Especially since I don't have a straightjacket available."

"I'm serious," I said. "I need your help. What does this have to do with the Code to Happiness?"

A half dozen DΣLPHI patrons stared up from their coffee and newspapers.

"Come over here," said Sophie, grabbing me by the elbow and ushering me to a corner littered with the crumbs, cups, and puddles of a hurried breakfast.

She held tightly to my elbow. Her eyes grew deep with intensity. A faint, ambiguous look that on Mona Lisa would pass for a smile tweaked her lips.

She shook her head disapprovingly. "Don't make a scene!"

"I'm not making a scene!"

"Yeah. Take a look around."

I looked and could see a number of DΣLPHI patrons staring at me.

"I'm sorry," I said, softening my appeal. "But I'd like to know. This is something important, isn't it?"

"Hope?" she said. "Of course."

"I mean, this thing…this *bronze* object," I said. "Please. I don't have much time. Not today, at least. Eddie's game is starting soon. Can't you give me a simple explanation?"

My head was reeling as I left the DΣLPHI Café. I had squeezed just enough from Sophie to fan my curiosity. There was more to the Code than I had imagined. That was clear now. But with Eddie's game at hand, I had little time to ponder the possibilities.

Slow Saturday traffic clogged the city arteries. As I dodged in and out of the gridlock, I tried to review and sort the elements – the symbols, the amulet's ornate design. What was significant? What was sheer ornament? How was I to tell?

And what was I to make of "hope"? How did it factor into this puzzle of human happiness? And how did it tie into everything that I had encountered and learned in recent weeks?

Of course, Sophie had once again been annoyingly less direct than I would have preferred. I had pressed her for answers, but she had been her typical evasive self. That was her way, and by now I was sure there was method to it. Her arcane messages were always mixed with her teasing charm. But she had acknowledged enough that I could ascertain that there was something to this Hope amulet.

I thought back over her remarks. She had left a few clues, hadn't she? Remember them now. Decipher them later.

I glanced at my watch. Not much time before kickoff. I swung the car off of Madison Street and took a weaving shortcut through a residential area.

Traffic had clogged the area near the stadium. I parked the car hurriedly and ran the four remaining blocks to the stadium. I was a bit disheveled and out of breath when I arrived at the gate.

But I was there.

The marching band drew a roar from the crowd as it exploded with the sound of the Exley High School fight song. The blare of brass over a pulsing bass drum brought the fans to their feet. Hundreds of fans had stopped near the north end zone to give a grand ovation to the Exley Eagles. I sidled to the nearest bleachers and stepped up on the first bench to see if I could spot Randy and Carrie in the stands. As I scoured the center sections, I saw Randy rise from his seat and wave. I waved back and headed their way.

The snare drums broke into a gattling rap that signaled the explosion of the Exley squad from the north tunnel. Eddie and his phalanx of receivers trailed most of the red-shirted Eagles. An extra cheer climbed above the roar when the fans spotted their neat, coordinated canter.

"Quite a crowd," I said as I slid into the tight patch of bench between Randy and Carrie.

No game in years had attracted the attention of this match with Carter Academy. Heated rivals even when they sported the most tepid teams, both schools were fielding their best squads in decades.

Everyone expected an exciting game. Both defenses were big, tough, and hard-hitting, and each offense could put a lot of points on the board. The Carter offense was built around a fearsome running game. Exley's advantage was a scintillating passing attack led by Eddie and a trio of receivers with foot-speed aplenty: Winston Marquardt, Billy James, and Tony Trillo.

Exley won the coin toss and elected to receive. By the time the Carter place kicker booted the ball high and end over end, the entire crowd was on its feet.

Tony Trillo gathered in the ball at the Exley 10-yard line. He broke, light-footed, toward a wall of four blockers to his left, found an opening as the red and white jerseys collided in a loud mass of color. He cut back to the center of the seemingly open field when a white-clad Cougar came from nowhere. His vicious hit on Trillo sent shockwaves through the afternoon air.

The tone was set.

Eddie, wearing his familiar number 8, and the rest of the Exley offense took the field.

"Do you think he's ready for this?" Carrie asked as the team huddled.

"Frankly, I think he was born for this," I said as the Exley huddle broke with a clap.

Seconds later, I felt like a prophet as Eddie barked the signals, dropped back five quick steps, pump-faked and fired a long strike down the right sideline. Billy James took it in over his shoulder at full stride and, stepping through the grasping hands of the falling safety, galloped into the end zone. Pandemonium reigned on the Exley side of the field.

We were on our way.

Or so it seemed.

Carter took possession on its 25-yard line and proceeded to march downfield and score another touchdown of their own.

"I don't know if I can take this for a full game!" said Carrie as the Carter fans cheered across the field.

"Pace yourself," I hollered back. "It's only the first quarter."

The game transformed into a chess match in the second quarter, with lots of action between the 20-yard lines. But timely defensive plays or untimely penalties stalled each drive before either team could notch a score. Exley scored a field goal in the remaining moments of the second quarter to take a 10-7 lead. Both teams headed for their locker rooms knowing that the game was a far cry from over.

A drum roll from the marching band was punctuated by the second half kick-off.

The game remained a defensive struggle for the next several series. Neither offense could mount a threat. Carrie pressed her fist against her mouth from time to time. She had nervous worry written across her face.

The day was big, its details painted with bold brushstrokes and heightened with anthems and rhythms and raw emotion. I wondered if Eddie could continue to focus and keep it all together in this, the biggest game of his young life.

Carter scored another touchdown behind the relentless ground attack of Fulmer and Williams. Carter's defense toughened as the game clock ticked off precious minutes. At the end of the 3rd quarter, Carter was ahead by 4 points. Exley fans were getting nervous.

The 4th quarter saw the teams battle back and forth without a change in the score. Time was running out.

With only two minutes left in the game, the Exley team huddled around Coach Riley. After the timeout, the team headed straight to the line of scrimmage, surprising the Carter defense. Eddie barked a single count and, with a three-step drop, lofted the ball toward Tony Trillo, who secured it with the fingertips before getting bumped out of bounds. The play was good for twenty yards. Again without a huddle, Eddie took the snap and dumped a short pass to Trillo coming out of the backfield. The play earned Exley another first down, but, with the ball in the middle of the field, it had used up valuable seconds on the clock.

With a minute remaining in the game, Exley called its last timeout.

With the outcome of the season riding on each play, the atmosphere had grown electric.

Eddie slightly overthrew Marquardt on the next play, and the ball bounced off the receiver's fingertips in the left flat.

Randy elbowed me hard. "Win should have had that," he exclaimed.

"I don't know," I said. "Tough catch to make."

"Come on, Eddie," Carrie shouted.

Eddie rolled to his right on the next play and found Billy James breaking free of his defender. Eddie fired a perfect strike to James, but the ball caromed off his chest and wobbled drunkenly toward the sidelines. The whole stadium could sense the pain, embarrassment, and disappointment behind James' facemask.

"Shake if off, Billy," Carrie hollered.

And shake it off they did. Eddie, leading his teammates, hit three quick strikes in a row, driving the ball all the way down to the 12-yard line. There was precious little time remaining on the clock. In seconds, elation and disappointment would flow from opposite sides of the great divide of outcome. Waves of wonder and worry and excitement flooded the stadium as the team huddled for one final play. Nothing short of a touchdown mattered.

The referee's whistle put the world in motion once again. Eddie barked the count. He felt the pressure from the right side of the Carter line and glided to his own right as his receivers drew white shirts like magnets. Eddie faked toward the far corner of the end zone and disappeared under a pair of Carter linemen. Miraculously, the football flew, catapulted from the huge mound of uniforms collapsing upon Eddie.

The ball headed toward the tall target of Winston Marquardt on the opposite side of the field. As the gun sounded, Marquardt adjusted to the outside, away from the hurtling defender, his hands zeroing in on the only object in the world that then mattered.

The football reached his hands at the precise instant the fingertips of the Carter cornerback crossed his path. The ball struck the receiver's hand, high off an index finger, and bounded away.

Marquardt looked up from the grass and watched the ball roll dead at the five-yard line.

The stadium emptied like a bag of breakfast cereal. Carrie had sought out Eddie as he came off the field, mute and dejected. His disappointment was obvious. He turned from her abruptly as she offered consolation. Coach Riley saved her from an awkward interlude as he herded his players to the locker room and a farewell for a season turned suddenly bittersweet.

"Why don't you two head home," I said. "I think Eddie's going to need a while to unwind. Let's give him some space."

Carrie started to protest, then thought better of it as Randy placed a hand in the middle of her back and led her to the parking lot.

I waited at the midfield tunnel, thinking about the game and the mix of glory and disappointment that came with it. An Exley banner lay abandoned on the ground, the bright crimson seeming to dim with the fading day. I picked it up, tucked it under my arm, and headed back toward the locker room.

I heard talking. The voices carried like cries in a canyon. I speculated that one was Coach Riley's. Even through a muffled response, I knew the other all too well.

"Heads up now. You had a monster day!"

"Yeah, sure."

I stopped before I reached the end of the tunnel. Though vaguely familiar, the voice was not Riley's after all.

"We lost," said Eddie.

"Lost what?"

"What do you mean? We lost the game. You saw it."

"Oh, yeah. I saw the game. I just didn't see any losers out there. Especially not Number 8."

"Well, check the scoreboard next time. You may be in for a surprise," Eddie said.

His bitterness cracked the air like a whip. I hung out from the edge of the wall, out of sight.

The voice continued in spite of Eddie's apparent disinterest. "Good things happen. Bad things happen. Doesn't mean a thing. One person's success is another's failure. A failure may be a step to success. Wins? Losses? In the end, there's only one scoreboard worth looking at."

"I don't follow you."

"All kinds of things happen on the outside. All that matters is on the inside. Thomas Edison failed a thousand times while trying to invent the light bulb. He never saw things that way, though. No, he believed he had discovered a thousand ways *not* to make an electric light. He was so fixed on his mission, so intent on his invention, that he simply refused to let results that others would call failure frustrate him."

"Yeah, well, they don't give you another chance on the last play of a football game. Maybe if they put a game clock on inventions, Edison would have wilted, too."

"Is that what you did, Eddie? Did you wilt?"

"I didn't make the play. Carter's defensive back tipped it away, didn't he?"

"I saw a pass that was right on the money, less than an inch from completion. A game of inches. That's what football is. But you can really say the same thing about most games, especially the most important game of all."

"What's that?" asked Eddie.

"The game of life."

Eddie said nothing. His feet shuffled uncomfortably.

The speaker went on.

"We can't control a lot of things in life. That's not true of attitude, though. We may not have a choice about certain facts of our lives or outcomes. We may not have much choice about what other people feel or do. But we have a choice about how we elect to act and feel about what goes on around us. More importantly, we have a choice about how we feel about *ourselves* and how we feel about others.

"Our attitude is more important than looks, brains, or athletic skills. It's more important than a silver tongue. Often, the key to getting what we're after, doing what we want to do, is just a matter of focus and desire. And those, young man, come from what we can conjure up from deep within."

"So what are you saying? I didn't want it enough?"

"From where I was sitting, it looked like you wanted this game as much – or more – than any fellow out there today. In fact, I was impressed with how you picked yourself up after big hits and kept your poise under pressure. I was even more impressed with how you seemed to inspire the rest of the team for that comeback. You motivated them, Eddie. Your will, your enthusiasm was the difference. And it almost – almost – changed the outcome of this game."

"But it didn't," Eddie retorted, unconvinced. "What's the difference between coming up short in the final seconds and getting beat by 42 points?"

"Did you ever hear of Stephen Hawking?"

"Yeah. I think so. Wasn't he some kind of genius? A rocket scientist or something?"

"Close. Many people think he has done the most brilliant theoretical work in science since Einstein. But he can't walk, can barely move at all without some kind of assistance. He can't sign his name or even talk without a mechanical voice simulator. He uses an optically activated computer system to compose his books because he can't write or type." He paused to let the point sink in.

"The amazing thing, though, is that virtually all of his best work has come since he contracted ALS, what we call Lou Gehrig's disease," he continued. "Many people pity him. But Hawking himself wonders if he ever would have made such dramatic accomplishments without the disease. He believes the condition made him focus and find meaning in the life he was left to live with the onset of the debilitating disease. He could have pitied himself, given up. Instead he used each step of his physical decline to climb to greatness."

"Yeah, but that guy is a genius. What you're really saying is that the rest of us should just fool ourselves. Pretend that we won when we really lost. I mean, shouldn't you face the truth? Shouldn't we be realists instead of fooling ourselves?"

"Eddie. Games are just that – games. They are created to bring out our best efforts. They are just shells for what takes place inside the participants and even inside the spectators. A focus on winning is really a focus on giving the best possible performance. Without measure, we can't reach for something greater. More than winning or losing is what we *become* in the course of our endeavors. And we can choose to appreciate the experience and its lessons or simply choose to be disappointed, especially when we don't get what we want. How we choose is the real test of greatness."

There it was again. That word. Appreciation. Its breadth of meaning was obviously far wider than I had previously considered. I strained to hear the rest of the conversation.

"Remember, Eddie. They're all games of inches. The difference in your game was a fragment of a defender's finger. Could you have thrown a better pass? Maybe, but not by much. Besides, we have no guarantee that Winston would have caught it, do we?"

Silence followed. I wondered what was passing through Eddie's mind.

Finally he spoke.

"But what's the point of it? I mean, what does it really matter? Nothing changes. The score's the same. Any way you cut it, Exley loses. I go back to school on Monday. What's the difference if I'm bummed out and angry, or I 'make the most out of it,' as you say."

"Hope," he said. "Hope is what matters. If you want to lead a rich, happy life, Eddie, you have to feed hope."

"Big deal," said Eddie. "I hope we win the state championship next season. I hope I get a car when I get my driver's license. Very big deal. It means nothing."

"That's not what I mean Eddie," he said. "It's hope that gets us through the toughest times. And it is hope that leads us forward and opens the door to our happiness. Happiness follows only in the wake of hope. You have a long life ahead, Eddie. Fill it with hope."

"And how do I do that?" Eddie asked.

"Appreciation, Eddie. It's all in the ability to appreciate how beautiful the world is, even when it doesn't seem so beautiful. Whether we do this through a sense of humor or optimism or stepping back and trying to take perspective on the bigger picture that may be lurking out there. It's not about pretending everything is great, but about finding what is great in the world, or in our lives, and savor that.

"Now comes the moment of real truth," he continued. "Will you draw something positive from today? Will you find motivation for next year? Will you appreciate what the team accomplished this season? Will you remember what it was like to play as a team, to *be* a team?

"Of course, you have other choices, too. You can blame yourself. You can blame your teammates or the referees. You can give up your dreams and save yourself from this brand of disappointment again."

The two speakers moved away, and as I stood there in silence, it dawned on me.

These lessons about loss and disappointment were mine as well as Eddie's.

I walked casually into the tunnel, feeling strange for having eavesdropped for so long, but glad to have heard and witnessed the exchange. I smiled at Eddie, who, now alone, conjured a faint smile in return. I peered to the far end of the tunnel where a tall man's silhouette broke from the shadows. He looked over his shoulder.

The stranger, who I could not positively identify, nodded to us both. At first, I thought he looked like Paul Minitauer, and I was about to call out. But then I took another look and knew I must be mistaken. The silhouette, the walk, reminded me of someone else I knew.

Someone who lay in a hospital bed at that very instant.

The Socrates Smith Notebook

"When the great scorer comes to write against your name, he marks not that you won or lost, but how you played the game."
    -Grantland Rice

"You'll always miss 100% of the shots you don't take."
    -Wayne Gretzky

"A ship in a harbor is safe, but that is not what ships are built for."
    -John Shedd

"Character consists of what you do on the third and fourth tries."
    -James A. Michener

"If you cry because the sun has gone out of your life, your tears will prevent you from seeing the stars."
    -Rabindranath Tagore

"In times like these, it helps to recall that there have always been times like these."
   -Paul Harvey

"If you don't like something, change it. If you can't change it, change your attitude. Don't complain."
   -Maya Angelou

"One of the things I learned the hard way was that it doesn't pay to get discouraged. Keeping busy and making optimism a way of life can restore your faith in yourself."
   -Lucille Ball

"I always remember an epitaph which is in the cemetery at Tombstone, Arizona. It says: 'Here lies Jack Williams. He done his dammedest.' I think that is the greatest epitaph a man can have."
   -Harry S. Truman

CHAPTER TEN

THE AMULET

George Niketopoulous shuffled animatedly between the cash register and the cook's counter, lost and bewildered.

"Where is she?" I asked.

"Where is she? I dunno. She don' call. She don' come," he complained. It appeared that George was having another one of his not infrequent panic attacks.

"That's unusual," I said, comparably confused...and disappointed to boot. In the wake of recent encounters, my hopes of coaxing more clues to the Code had climbed. Now I had to wait...and wonder about Sophie as well.

"Why she don' call?" George asked as he rang up a coffee and bagel for a man in UPS khakis. His eyes were fixed on me. "Two dollars, seventy-five cents, please...Never she don' call. Never she sick."

He was right. Sophie was a permanent fixture in the DΣLPHI Café, as integral to its ambience, as essential to its success as George himself. Forget the wall photos of celebrities, many of whom George had probably never met, and the garish posters of a Greece invented by tourism marketers. Take away George behind the counter and Sophie with a coffee urn, and the DΣLPHI became just another diner.

"Smith. Why she no call?" George insisted, hoping again to pry the impossible from me. "You smart man. You tell me. Why she no call today?"

"I wish I could tell you, George," I said. "Believe me, I do."

"She make me crazy," said George. "Maybe she have heart attack....Maybe..."

I cut him off before he could continue his pointless speculation. "Don't worry yourself, George," I said. "I'm sure she's fine. She'll probably come walking through the door any minute."

She didn't.

I waited for an hour. George continued to fret and speculate as to the calamities that might have befallen Sophie over the weekend. No words could assuage his fears, however, so I told him I'd drive by her home.

"Where does she live?" I asked.

"I don' know," said George.

George handed her a check every week. A search through his employee records listed a post office box for Sophie. Her permanent address was an apartment on Styx Street on the north end of the city.

I found a tiny strip mall at the location. No one working at the dry cleaners, Laundromat, or convenience store remembered when any apartment building *had* stood on the site.

At the convenience store, a man wearing a beret adorned with the fighting leprechaun logo of Notre Dame University interjected that, yes, an apartment building had stood on the site ten or more years ago.

"Only you, Sophie," I muttered on my way out the door. Sophie would show up, I assured myself as I headed back home. No need to worry prematurely. My ringing cell phone interrupted my thoughts. It was Carrie.

"They've taken your father into intensive care," she said nervously.

"I'll head to the hospital right away," I said.

A doctor met me outside the swinging doors of intensive care. Dad's vital signs had triggered an alarm, and the nurses had rushed him to the ward to monitor him better.

"He's stabilized," the doctor explained. "You can see him."

An oxygen mask covered Dad's nose and mouth. His chest inflated and fell almost mechanically. A dry rasping sound – half human, half machine – escaped from the mask.

"Hi, Dad," I whispered. "We love you." Not sure whether my dad had heard me or not, I sat beside his bed and cried.

After awhile, and once I was sure Dad was settled into a peaceful sleep, I took a walk in the hospital courtyard. Gradually, my head cleared, and I began to think about the kids, Carrie, and my project for Stover. Before I knew it, my thoughts returned to the amulet.

For days, it had nagged at me like a stubborn melody playing over and over in my head.

Before the game on Saturday, Sophie had acknowledged that different versions of a Hope amulet had surfaced across a number of cultures throughout history.

I understood that the chitchatting, wisecracking persona she flashed at the DΣLPHI was just the frosting on her character. I wondered how many patrons of the DΣLPHI Café had seen through the banter and flirtatious smile. To how many others had she opened the mysteries of man's universal goal?

She was serious and direct when she finally spoke.

The Hope amulet had a long history, much of it buried in myth, legend, and misunderstanding, she had explained. Its origins were uncertain, though most traced it back to antiquity. Different scholars traced the amulet to different sources. Scholars believed that there were at least three or four different amulets in existence, each unique.

Kings, emperors, and tribal leaders had worn it, but, despite the optimism its name inspired as a good luck charm, it had left a checkered record. Its purported power was to bring happiness, great happiness, to those who possessed it, but the stories of its power were full of puzzling outcomes, not always favorable to the charm's possessor. Bull-headed leaders and tyrants had dashed it against palace walls and hurled it into deep lakes in anger and frustration, claiming it was a sham and that it generated more misery than it did hope and happiness.

"What kind of hope charm makes you miserable?" I quipped. "I'd be ticked off, too."

Sophie looked at me as if I were hopeless and told me that some of the amulet's possessors had embraced it and passed it along to others with the hope of sharing its mysteries. She also hinted that its power might lay in offering direction, not simply in its possession.

"Another thing…it's big," she continued.

"You mean big, like important?"

"No, I mean big like in BIG," she said. "Every Hope amulet that I have heard of must have been a clunky thing to wear around your neck. Bigger than what you have."

"Do you think there are other pieces to this amulet?"

"I can't tell you that," she said. "Happy hunting, Mr. Smith." She grabbed me by the arm and ushered me to the door. "Enjoy the game."

Now I repeated her words to myself.

And then I wondered, if the Hope amulet was missing another piece, what did that piece say?

I yawned deeply as my car came to a halt at the stoplight. The hours at the hospital following a late night of effort on the Stover project had taken their toll. Dad had put on his signature smile, wry and ironic, shortly after awakening. But not even his faint smile could conceal the seriousness of his condition. All vital signs were stable as I left, however, and Dad was sleeping like a baby.

I pulled into a parking space several doors from the DΣLPHI.

The special Kona blend was strong and flavorful. I felt a shudder of new life. George waved me off when I reached for my billfold.

"The police, they can't look for Sophie," he said. "Too soon."

"I know. People forget to call into work or let people know where they are going all the time. She'll show up, George."

"Aye, Sophie…" He finished muttering his sentence in Greek. Then he looked up at me with his black eyes. The wrinkles near his temples resembled the veins on a drainage map.

"Smitha, you good man," he said.

The afternoon waned. The Stover project claimed my time and attention. I set to work on the pile of material lying on the desk in my library. I was deep in thought when I heard Carrie's voice approaching.

"Here he is," said Carrie, while walking into my library with the phone. She handed me the phone and ominously whispered, "Ellen."

"Hello, sweetheart," I said.

"Hi," said Ellen. Silence followed.

"What's up?" I asked.

"I'm thinking of dropping out of school, Dad."

"Whoa!" I said. "Wait a minute. I think I've missed something. Let's back up. What happened?"

"Nothing is going right, Dad."

"Explain," I said. "Take your time and explain."

"Dad, I just don't belong here."

It had been a bad week for Ellen. But her expectations had made it all the worse. Foremost on her mind were her grades. "My grade on the logic test was a C⁺, and I thought I had done really well." Besides the logic class, she was disappointed in two other grades. Her roommate's boyfriend had become a nearly permanent fixture in their dorm room, often tying up the already limited access to the bathroom and shower in the mornings. When she had confronted her roommate with the awkwardness of the situation, a beastly argument had ensued.

"Ellen, I can understand why you are frustrated, but I don't think dropping out of school is the answer. Let things cool off with your roommate. You two will figure it out. As to the grades, believe me, you'll survive. Why don't you go to the gym and get a workout? You'll feel better."

I tried every angle I knew to get her out of her funk. Ten minutes later, Ellen's resolution had softened to "We'll see."

"Let these be the best years of your life, kid," I encouraged as we were finishing up. "Smell the roses. Enjoy your youth!"

There was silence on the end of the line. I wished I could have reached through the phone and given her a hug.

Carrie listened patiently to the recap of my day.

"Do I have time for a run?" I asked.

"Looks like you need it," she said, kissing my cheek. "Go ahead. Dinner can wait."

My hands and face tingled with the cool autumn air. The run was exactly what I needed, and I charted a long course that would take me into the city.

The day's stress had me a little tight and winded, but I slowly began to hit my stride and feel better.

By the time I had covered the distance to the Quad, the stress had burned off like morning fog. With the fountain before me, I sprinted down one of the paths radiating from the pool. I faded into a jog as I rounded it, then into a walk, hands on hips, gulping air greedily.

The run had invigorated me. The soft light of late afternoon created patches of gold between the shadows across the Quad. I jumped up on a stone bench beside the fountain and looked around. What a mix of wonder, joy, challenge, and even sadness my life had presented me. What meaning did "happiness" have at times like this? I could not separate any of it from this glorious afternoon, the satisfaction of a good run, my aching lungs, and the crisp bite of autumn.

I jumped from my perch and thought back to my evening with Minitauer a week before. I retraced my steps near our meeting place and stared at the ground where I had found the second piece of the Hope amulet. Its wide arc and ragged edges hinted that there were more pieces to the charm. Where had Minitauer found the piece, and why had he left its mate near the site of our meeting that night?

I walked the outer ring of the fountain center, searching the ground and everything around me for another sign. Not finding any new clues after having circled the area a second time, I took off at a dead run.

Darkness was settling in as I reached Minitauer's gate. The house appeared empty. The only light emanating from it was the dull yellow porch light. I opened the gate and headed toward the porch.

A note hung on a thumbtack pressed into the doorframe. My name was on it in large capital letters. I opened the note and read.

Smith –

Pardon my presumption, but I thought you'd be back. Had to leave town. Sorry we won't be able to pick up our discussion for a while.

In the meantime, I suggest that you head over to the museum for a "stark" impression of this matter.

Minitauer

The museum had been closed for hours, but I chanced a check.

Amber light flooded the cascading steps and the parking lot, but the building itself, with its colonial classicism, lay back in the shadows. The Museum of History and Art had been a welcome addition to our town's cultural milieu for about 10 years now. The city had acquired the old county building that once had seemed destined for demolition but had now been given a new lease on life. I was happy to see the building looking clean and well maintained. Dim security lights cast a gray light within.

I followed the walkway around the perimeter of the building, searching for some sign of human activity. A light shone from the window of a single-story addition. I went over to investigate.

Pushing through the lilac bushes beside the window, I felt like a thief. I caught a foothold in the boulder brick and managed to lift myself up just enough to see into the chamber. A pale woman, her hair tucked into a tight bun, sat hunched over a table full of objects. I gathered gumption for a moment and rapped on the window. She sat upright with a puzzled look. I rapped again, and she marched curiously toward the window, cupped her hands at the corners of her eyes and peered directly at me. I bent backward from the window ledge for a viewing angle. A moment of alarm flashed through her eyes when she finally focused on my straining torso.

"Can I speak with you?" I blurted.

She strained again to see me more clearly and, no doubt, determine if I was a threat to her safety.

"Please!" I shouted, as loud as I thought I could manage without sounding alarming. "Can I speak to you?" I grabbed a corner of the window ledge across my body with my left hand and gestured emphatically toward the back door with my right.

She puzzled further. "We're closed," she said.

"I know. But I have something you may find interesting."

She hesitated further. I reached into my pocket and stuck a piece of the amulet against the window. Her eyes widened. She looked me over once again, then headed toward the back door.

The door opened cautiously. All I could see was an eye and a patch of her hair, dark streaks beneath silver filaments.

"Who are you?" she asked.

"Smith," I said. I could see immediately that the name had made her only more wary. So I chanced it. "Socrates Smith," I said, letting the name hang in the night before I spoke again. "I need your assistance."

Apparently, I had picked the right moment to test the name's leverage.

"I shouldn't be doing this," she said. The door opened only inches more. My nose bumped the door as I squeezed through.

"And your name is…?" I paused, and I could see her apprehension grow again.

"Professor Stark," she said. "Mr.…Mr. Smith did you say?"

"Yes," I said, and we stood staring at each other for awkward seconds. I pulled out the pieces of the bronze amulet. She grabbed them from my hand, and her wariness dissolved.

"Where did you get this?" she asked.

"It's a long story."

"I've held three Hope amulets," said Professor Stark as she carefully scrutinized my specimen. "The oldest was at least 2200 years old with Greek lettering. The youngest and most elegant was made in Italy during the High Renaissance. Faultless craftsmanship, inexpressibly rich in design and materials." She pointed with a pen to the yellow topaz. "This one has an incredible array of jewels. It may be the youngest specimen yet."

"How recent?" I asked.

"I can't say for sure without running some tests. Maybe three hundred years old." She surveyed the broken edges. "One thing does distinguish this one though. Without a doubt it is in the worst condition. From the looks of these edges, it was broken deliberately."

"Why?"

"Who knows? Greed would usually be my first answer to anything of this nature. But the value would no doubt have been greater with the amulet intact. Besides, they left at least two of the jewels."

"What do you know about its history?" I asked.

"The history is spotty. I've found a number of indirect references to it and to those who have worn it. Most of the rest is legend. It's supposed to bring peace and happiness to the wearer. But a number of the references imply that many who wore it ended up disappointed…disillusioned."

"So I've heard," I said.

"I have always suspected its purpose was more informational than magical," she said.

"In what way?"

"Perhaps it was part of a puzzle."

"Or key to a secret code?" I asked.

She looked up at me with interest. "Yes, maybe," she said.

Professor Stark led me back to a laboratory. It was eclectically equipped, with manual microscopes that must have been 40 or more years old beside powerful electron magnification systems, assay devices, and other laboratory tools I couldn't identify. She grabbed a large magnifying glass, a la Sherlock Holmes, and set it over Minitauer's specimen.

"What do you make of all this?" I asked her some time later.

"I would have to do far more research to give you any definitive answer on its origin." I could sense her professional hunger.

"That's not what I'm asking, Professor. What do you think this Hope amulet is really about?"

She pondered the question.

"If you look back to the earliest creations of mankind, you'll find objects and images intended to direct the course of events – for good or evil," she began. "Often these objects were given to a child or special friend upon the bearer's death in order to transmit some of the power or knowledge they had learned so that future generations would benefit from…"

"But what do you think of the Hope amulet?" I interrupted. "Do you believe it holds the key to human happiness?"

She hesitated.

"If you are asking for my non-professional opinion, I believe that mankind has tried countless ways to communicate life's most cherished secrets. This amulet may offer the power of insight. Yes. That is possible."

I let her continue her examination without interruption. It was several minutes before she spoke again.

"Well, Mr. Smith, despite its condition, this is quite a find," said Professor Stark. "Forgive me my selfish interests, but I must ask…what are you going to do with this amulet?"

"Professor, I am not really interested right now in parlaying this amulet into fortune or fame, if that's your concern," I answered. "Trust me. I may well be able to offer it to you and the museum sometime in the future – perhaps the not too distant future at that. But first I need to find out what it's all about. The amulet holds something of value – enormous value, I believe – beyond the price of its gems or its worth as an artifact. I need to figure that out first." I could sense her apprehension about the ultimate fate of the amulet. So I added reassuringly: "I would love your help while I conduct this search."

She nodded and a smile broke across her face.

"I'd be glad to help," she said.

The clock tower across the parkway registered 11:30 as I left the museum. I looked down at my feet and realized that I was still wearing my running clothes. Carrie's dinner had been waiting longer than I had realized or had intended. I had completely lost track of time.

That seemed to be the pattern these days. I rushed home as fast as I could.

Carrie was sleeping on the couch when I arrived. An open book straddled her chest. She stirred when I kissed her forehead twice, then she settled back to sleep.

I cleared my desk in the library and set the pieces of the amulet before me.

What is hope anyway? I considered its meaning. Is it not the light of promise and possibility? Hope keeps the spirit alive amid sickness and disaster, failure and loss, and even in times of danger.

Hope welcomes the future while giving life to the present.

And in this strange hour, what better embodiment of hope did I have than Dad, ever the fisherman, finding hope in every cast?

The Socrates Smith Notebook

Happiness includes adapting to life - and all the curve balls thrown our way. We cannot eliminate life's challenges and unpleasantness, but we can grow and become greater spirits through crisis, sadness, misfortune, disappointment, failure, and even tragedy.

The happiness I believe we seek is fulfillment, a sense of serenity, and the feeling of being whole and connected.

Pleasure may be fleeting. Pleasure wanes once it finds its object. We exhaust it, wear it out, and dull its impact.

Happiness, on the other hand, is something deeper. It is fulfillment, inner joy, and satisfaction. It may linger even after attendant pleasure has passed. Ideally, it is free from the pettiness, fear, greed, and the other unsettling emotions that generate human misery.

"If you really want to be happy, no one can stop you."
    -Sister Mary Tricky

"Live a life as a monument to your soul."
    -Ayn Rand

"The tragedy of life is not so much as what men suffer, but rather what they miss."
    -Thomas Carlyle

"Life is a great big canvas; throw all the paint you can at it."
    -Danny Kaye

"A person will be called to account on Judgment Day for every permissible thing he might have enjoyed but did not."
-The Talmud

"Since the house is on fire, let us warm ourselves."
-Italian proverb

"Better to light a candle than to curse the darkness."
-Chinese proverb

"The grand essentials of happiness are something to do, something to love and something to hope for."
-Allan K. Chalmers

CHAPTER ELEVEN

FIRST SECRETS

"What are you up to, Dad?" Randy asked. His head hovered in space at the edge of the doorway to my library. I was back at work on the Stover project. I had given Phillip my report a few days earlier, but there were some additional items I wanted to look into. I'd do those on my nickel, and, if I came up with anything good, I'd share it with him.

"Just thinking," I said.

"Yeah," he snickered. "For a change."

"Right. What are you up to?" I asked.

He shuffled for a moment, digging for words.

"I don't think I'm going to jump on that recording contract after all. It's enticing, but I think you were right. Things are coming together. We're doing more gigs. No sense tying ourselves into a one-sided contract."

"I think that's the right call, Randy. Keep the faith. You'll make the right decision when the time comes."

"Yeah," he said, head bobbing in thought.

He tapped out a quick rhythm on the door jamb and disappeared.

I decided to take a break from my work and focus, instead, on wrapping up a few loose ends of bills and family business.

The warbling of the telephone interrupted my musing. It was Josephine. Before I could register her identity, she had connected me with Phillip Stover.

"I'm very impressed, Smith," he said. "You outdid yourself with this report."

"Thanks, Phillip."

"No, thank *you*. I was confident that you could handle this assignment. I hadn't counted on such depth in the interviews or such insightful analysis. I'm really impressed."

"I enjoyed the project," I said, not realizing how much I missed the old office pat on the back. "Let me know if you have any questions you'd like to discuss. I have some other ideas I may follow up on with you."

Stover said that he had his bearings now. The report gave him a good sense of what he could expect from his workers – and demand from the plant over the next six months.

"I also have a pretty good idea of where we'll find the real battleground," he added. I knew immediately what he had in mind. Discontent had followed the acquisition, and despite the best of intentions, Stover and his team had met stubborn resistance at almost every critical juncture. The plan I had laid out in my report provided a roadmap for Stover's mission.

I couldn't help but admire his handling of the situation. Instead of cutting the workforce along with his contrary lieutenants – a quick, easy, and, under the circumstances, justifiable fix – Phillip saw an opportunity to build a real team, to make converts of the doubters.

I had become a fan of Stover and his business philosophy. Stover saw a chance to boost both confidence and profitability with a few timely measures, and, along the way, improve morale. So much did I want his effort to succeed that I had had to caution myself against allowing bias to filter into my report. I was confident that I had been as objective as possible.

I had really enjoyed the team-building work. As I thought about it, the opportunity to help people to work effectively together bore similarities to my insights into happiness.

Phillip had hinted that he might have other projects for me, and encouraged me to explore the possibilities of a new career centered around team building exercises. Certainly there were other companies with similar needs. "You bring plenty to the party, Smith," he had complimented.

The project had lifted my hopes and magnified my job opportunities beyond all prior expectations. Still, something beyond the project itself and Phillip's praise had elevated my spirit. The project had enlightened me to some broader truths. Basing his decision on core principles and a clear understanding of his goals rather than expediency had made Phillip's decisions and path forward clear despite the challenges and difficulties they posed. Most people, Stover explained, never stop to even appreciate what their core principles and values are.

In the few short weeks of the project, we had identified easy to implement small changes to improve team morale, such as modest realignment of work responsibilities. By solving easier issues first – the proverbial "low-hanging fruit" – Stover hoped to gain momentum to take on the tougher issues later.

My thoughts, like cogs in one of the plant's new machines, began to engage one another and move in a new direction. I reached for a sweater and went for a walk around the block.

My mind kept churning as I tried to clarify the ideas that were swimming around in my head. Focus on opportunities, not problems. Stay true to your values and principles. Themes I had encountered at work and in books many times before. But I had never stopped to think of how these themes might be related. Now I did. And then a thought lit up my brain.

Eureka! I turned towards home and walked as quickly as I could. Heading straight to the library, I opened *The Socrates Smith Notebook* and jotted several lines down.

> *The secret is to focus on –*
> · *High impact*
> · *Opportunities (rather than problems). Always act from your*
> · *Principles (rather than expediency) and choose to work first on areas that are*
> · *Easy to resolve or put into effect so as to build momentum for ongoing initiatives.*

I looked at my notebook with the rush that comes with new understanding. As if to prove what I already knew, I took my pen and circled the first letters from each of these key points. The word *HOPE* was unmistakable.

My mind abruptly shifted gears again. I thought about my recently adopted workout schedule. I had started with a mile run and had gradually increased it. Someone else might have started out with a fast – or even slow – walk. And someone else's health regimen, thinking of my conversation with Dr. Ortiz, might have started out altogether differently, perhaps with a resolve to eat healthier foods or to get more sleep. Hope represented more than an attitude. It also seemed to offer direction.

The phone rang. I answered it, trying hard not to lose my stream of consciousness. It was Ellen.

Ellen announced that she was coming home. When I asked about school, silence crept over the phone like a thick fog.

"I'm so unhappy, Dad," she said.

Relying on parental instinct, I chose not to dissuade her. "I'm looking forward to seeing you, El. Take your time and be careful. I love you." I hung up the phone, concerned about my daughter's well-being and wondering what, if anything, I could do to help her.

Knowing that Ellen wouldn't be home for awhile, and with an empty house, I decided to get a cup of coffee. Perhaps Sophie had returned, and I could test my new thoughts out on her. I felt I was close, perhaps now having unlocked a part of the Code to Happiness. I was anxious to share any helpful insights on improving attitude with Ellen, who so desperately could use a new perspective. A new sense of hope.

George was working the cash register when I walked into the DƐLPHI. He threw his hands up, as if to answer my question before I could ask it.

"See. She was here," he said, holding up a red scarf. I nodded as if to confirm it might have been Sophie's. "But where is she? Do you believa this, Smith?"

"Do you want to check in with the police?" I asked.

"No," George said abruptly. "She not dead. She just don't think about George. I wait till she call me. I don' look for her no more."

"I'm sure there's a reason, George," I said.

"Sure. Make me crazy. That good reason for Sophie."

"Hang in there, George," I said.

I briefly thought of stopping at the police station, but I suspected that George was right. Sophie's disappearance was strange and unprecedented, but I think we both had come to expect the unexpected from Sophie.

The street vendors were out en masse – hot dog and pretzel stands, coffee wagons and soft drink carts, and, of course, the news stands with their curious mix of literature. A street guitarist played to a fast-paced crowd too busy to stop and listen to his words.

I drove along Charles Street, turned on the boulevard at Center City. In an almost dizzying rush, fatigue swept over me. One event had piled upon another and then another, and now I was feeling the load. I had been a perpetual motion machine of late. I was anticipating Ellen's arrival home as well as bad news from the hospital. In spite of the coffee, I still felt tired.

I decided to make a beeline for the Quad and find a place to relax. I recalled Minitauer's comments about a labyrinth as a spiritual place designed for quiet meditation. I wasn't feeling all that spiritual, but the idea of finding a quiet moment in the day sure sounded appealing. I parked and headed toward the fountain.

The city sparkled with the cool, fresh air and brilliant blue of a crisp autumn day. A cold front had passed with the prior evening's rain, and the cobblestone paths were clean and bright and buzzing with people. The walk and fresh air did wonders for body and soul, and I was thankful for the beauty of the day.

I closed my eyes. The fall sun fell weakly on my face. A gust of wind touched my cheek and hands, brushed the folds in my pants.

"Breathe in the beauty," a soft voice said.

"Yes," I answered dreamily before realizing that the voice was not the product of my own mind.

Beside me stood an attractive, dark-haired woman. She had thin, well-defined eyebrows and wore a long sari rich with blue and violet trim. She seemed vaguely familiar, but it was her look of profound serenity that drew my attention.

We silently watched the fountain for a few moments before the strange woman began to speak. She introduced herself by telling me her name was Serena. I responded by telling her only my last name, Smith.

"My mother used to say that you can live an entire life in a single moment," she said.

I tried to size this woman up but couldn't.

"What do you think she meant?" I asked.

"That a moment is too precious to waste," she replied. "It carries all that has come before, and it bears the seed of tomorrow. But above all, we should love it because the moment is all that we really have."

What she had said struck me as true, though not something we tend to focus on much. Taking the time to simply be conscious of living in the moment was becoming a lost art.

She was comfortable with the long silence that followed our exchange. She neither hurried nor attempted to persuade me when she spoke again.

"We need to clear the mind of clutter. Clear the mind of noise," she said.

It did seem ironic. With all the new technology designed to make our lives easier – cell phones, e-mails, faxes, and remote controls that allowed us to surf 500 television channels in the span of a commercial – the world had, indeed, become a noisy and very busy place. More complicated in many ways, not easier. Taking the time to enjoy nature or to simply sit down to an old-fashioned family dinner seemed a lost luxury.

But Serena hadn't finished.

"The problem with today's clutter is that it crowds out room for the most important things in life. The things that really matter."

"Such as?" I replied.

"Such as love. Think about it. What is the first ingredient of love?" she asked. She seemed to take delight in asking the question. Her eyes sparkled, as if they were inlaid with jewels.

"I don't know," I laughed.

She squeezed my arm tightly, gave it a shuddering shake. "Come on, now," she said imploringly.

She was insistent but patient. She gently folded her small hands together and waited for my response.

"Attention?" I finally replied after thinking for a moment.

She relaxed her grip. "Of course. Attention! Nothing can be loved unless it has our attention. Nor can we love without giving the object of love our attention. And that's hard to give if we're too busy on our cell phones or glued to the television or computer."

From first dawn to last light, heightened attention is the first spark of love, Serena explained. It brings the object of love into bright focus, making that object accessible to our mind and our emotions even after it has left our physical presence. In memory and emotion, we carry it with us.

"And for love to evolve and grow, attention must always remain at its core," she said.

The theme was familiar. Carrie was fond of quoting the anonymous line that "love is a verb." And I agreed that, as a verb, love required action. Even to love our car – an object incapable of returning our love with like emotion – is to give it attention in the form of cleaning and maintenance. Loving another human being certainly required no less action!

"I understand your point," I said. "But how does this relate to taking the time to enjoy the present?"

"Living in the moment is living mindfully, with awareness and appreciation," she said. "Each moment offers us some gift of lesson or beauty. To give our attention and appreciation to each moment is the first step to bringing love into the fabric of our lives."

Questions, one after another, arose in my mind. But they all slipped away with her next words.

"Love," said Serena quietly, "is the cement of the happy life."

Serena had grabbed my attention in a strange and timely way. I was growing accustomed to such encounters, and sometimes I felt like Alice, seeing the world through a looking glass, more vividly and clearly than I had before. How much of my life, I wondered, had I lost to the dullness of inattention? How much more, I resolved, would I capture in the rest of my life!

We stared wordlessly at the fountain. Pigeons roosted on the rail. A pair of gulls drank from the elevated pool between shooting arcs of fountain water. Water fell like a curtain from the rim of the second basin to the main pool.

I had so much to say to Serena that I wasn't quite sure where to begin. I opted for simple and sincere. "Thank you, Serena." I sensed it was all that needed to be said.

She smiled, then quietly walked away. I watched her depart, and then, without turning to look back at me, she raised her hand and wiggled her fingers in a gesture of good-bye that conjured memories of someone else that I knew.

"So, she reminds you of someone, does she?" I would have known that voice anywhere.

"Sophie!" I said, turning around. And there stood the oracle, bright and brilliant and dressed in a gown of flowing white silk. The wind that was sending leaves dancing and crackling across the Quad had her gown waving like layers of silky flags.

Behind her ear was a red rose.

"Yes," I said, "she does remind me of someone." I spun around again and looked down the walkway. Serena had vanished. I stared back at Sophie, then down the path again and shook my head.

"Are you two related?" I asked, trying to sort the pieces together.

"She's my sister."

"Your sister?"

"Sure. Can't I have a sister like everyone else?"

"You're not like anyone else, Sophie!" I said.

She took several steps toward me and grabbed my cheek with her right hand, cupping my chin. "So you were worried about me, huh?"

I took her hand, and looked at it for a short moment. It was firm yet soft, without callous or blemish of any kind despite her years of work at the DΣLPHI. I was glad to see her again.

"Forget about me," I said. "George is worried sick. He's breaking out in those bumps again."

"Don't worry," she said wryly. "I'll take care of George."

"You shouldn't scare him like that," I said. "So tell me, woman of mischief and mystery, where *have* you been? George said you've never missed a day at the DΣLPHI before now."

"Seemed like it was time for a vacation," she said without elaboration.

"You could have said something."

"Sometimes people need to wonder a bit," she said.

"You're holding back," I said.

"I'm always holding something back!" she said. "You ought to know that by now. If I told you everything I know, there'd be nothing left to discover."

"I've had that sense lately," I said.

We sized each other up like two best friends from high school who were seeing each other at a reunion for the first time in twenty years. Finally, Sophie lifted a white bag.

"Thought you might be interested in this," she said, reaching into the bag.

Out came a chunk of black metal. I looked at it and immediately recognized it as part of the amulet. It had an inscription on its side which I deciphered as "HA."

"The amulet!" I shouted.

The piece was even larger than those I already possessed. On closer inspection, the letters HA lay in relief, having been set vertically, each in a gentle arc opposite the other and following the contour of what was clearly the original amulet's outer edge.

"I thought it was time to dig this up for you," she said.

"Where did you get it? What does it mean, 'HA'?" Without giving Sophie a chance to answer, I continued. "'HA.' I wonder…I've been thinking that laughter is important to happiness. Maybe the amulet is telling me that. Maybe the missing piece is another 'HA.' Or 'HA HA.' I can imagine a wise person making this charm thinking that if we can laugh at the trials and tribulations that come our way, not take life too seriously, we'll be happier."

"It took a fair amount of digging to come up with these," she said, avoiding the question. "Seems like you've needed more help than the last guy," she said.

"The last guy? Who was that?"

Again, she ignored my question.

"So is that why you disappeared?"

"That...and other things," she said, flashing a look that made it clear this part of the inquiry was over.

"Tell me more about the amulet," I implored.

"I could tell a lot of tales, but there is only one thing you need to know," she said. "It has probably frustrated more people than it has helped."

"Why is that?"

"Most have had misconceptions about it, about its purpose."

"And what is its purpose?" I asked.

"I have confidence in you, Socrates Smith," she said. "I am sure you will get it...even if you don't right now. I've believed in you all along."

She seemed bemused by my quizzical look, but continued. "The problem is human expectation. People want happiness to come to them. They don't want to work to create it."

She held up the piece again, admiring it like a fine piece of craft.

"I'm sure that's what Stover was talking about when he said money or things can't buy happiness," I said. "I'm beginning to understand that happiness is more a consequence of how we live than what we have. Maybe the point isn't to possess the amulet like a bottle of fine wine or a fancy car but to see its importance as a guide to living a good life?"

Again Sophie didn't answer. At least not directly. "The amulet does seem to have one real power."

"What's that?" I asked.

"The power to enchant," she said smiling. "It does make life more interesting when you're wondering about it. Right?"

"Yes," I laughed. "It certainly does."

I listened to Sophie and looked down to study the piece again when she was finished. Unlike the other pieces to the amulet, this was clean and polished, as if it had been well handled and had sat in a protected case.

"HA," I read again. "The other piece reads HOPE. What's the connection?"

"That's something for you to figure out."

Sophie was no help this time.

Sophie dropped the piece of the amulet into her bag and gave it to me to hold for safekeeping. Then, she took me by the arm, and we walked around the fountain.

"Love is a favorite topic in my family. Our specialty, you might say. There are four of us. Four sisters. Our mother gave each of us one of love's lessons. Serena's was to live in the moment. To Frieda, she gave openness."

"Openness?" I repeated. "Do you mean that to love, we have to make ourselves vulnerable?"

"That's part of it. But it need not be so dangerous or grueling as you make it sound. Openness does involve sacrifice, however. We must sacrifice our preconceptions, sometimes even attitudes that we cling to out of habit or laziness. Openness may require us to suspend judgment, to attempt to understand before we label, particularly when our impulse is to condemn.

"Listening. Learning. Loving. They are all alike in this regard. It is difficult to do either when our minds and hearts are closed."

Sophie stopped at the fountain and pointed to a pair of pigeons splashing in the fountain pool. "Opening your eyes makes a difference, too," she added.

"And the other two lessons? One of them must be yours."

"You're getting ahead of me," she said, slapping my arm. "To Golda, mother gave the lesson of value. Love imbues the thing we love with value. We identify that person or thing or idea as distinctive, as something special and worthy of the attention we give it. We pull it out from the complexities of life and define it with special status or importance.

"Self-respect, or what, today, we call self-esteem, also depends on valuing," she went on. "Without first valuing ourselves and our own lives, it is difficult, if not impossible, to love others. Self-esteem entails living with dignity, defining yourself as someone whose feelings, thoughts, and ideas matter."

What Sophie said resonated with my experience and the principles by which I tried to live. I was interested in hearing the final lesson.

"That leaves one," I said. "What lesson did your mother pass along to you?"

I detected the look of mischief even before she strung her arm through mine again, linking us tightly at the elbow. "Engagement," she said.

"Sophie, I'm spoken for," I teased.

"No, Smith. I mean engagement, as in connection, being committed and involved," she said. "Well, perhaps this one does need a little explaining. Fortunately, we Greeks have a lot of experience in this. Do you know anything about tragedy?"

"Do you mean death and disaster?"

"Yes. But I was thinking of the theater. We Greeks invented literary tragedy, you know."

"So I've heard."

"Well, beneath the conflict and fall in classic tragedy is a story of disconnection," she went on. "Take Macbeth's ambition or Othello's jealousy… all end in people being separated from those whom they should have loved most. In the end, they disconnect themselves from humanity."

"In contrast, the classic 'happy ending' finds folks reunited after conflict," I said. "Engaged like intermeshed gears. That's an interesting way to look at drama."

Sophie grew serious. "It's important to understanding love," she said, making sure I did not stray far from her point. "It's important to happiness. A rewarding life is shared. Life without love grows insulated and stale. Our ties to others, the sharing of our lives with others, are our links to happiness. Love is the most sincere form of appreciation. That's the real lesson my mother gave to her four daughters.

"I know that other people can grate on us. They can cause us problems and hurt us. And, yes, sometimes we have to move on, to move away from those whose influence is destructive and find others with whom we can share our lives more fruitfully. But life without love is life without luster. A life filled with love is satisfying and enriching," she said, staring out into the horizon, as if towards her mother. "Yes, we must share our lives and our love if we are going to be happy."

The house was empty when I arrived home. Randy had left a tape of his music playing. I was pleasantly surprised with the sound and with Randy's lyrics in particular. I owed him a compliment. I grabbed my notebook and plopped into my desk chair. The lessons of my meeting with Sophie were fresh, and I did not want to lose them.

"Do me one favor," I had said as we had parted. "Let George know you are all right."

"He'll be fine," she said. "He's probably found a replacement for me already."

"There's no replacing you, Sophie," I said. I meant it in more ways than I could express.

Then, I opened the pouch Sophie had given me and carefully took out the new piece to the Hope amulet. The charm contained the word, or at least, the letters

"HA." I stared at it, looking for meaning. But it stared back in silence, its meaning still a mystery waiting to be discovered.

The Socrates Smith Notebook

The 1st secret:
HOPE provides direction for action!

"You just don't luck into things as much as you'd like to think you do. You build step by step, whether it's friendship or opportunities."
   -Barbara Bush

"A journey of a thousand miles begins with a single step."
   -Chinese proverb

"Start by doing what's necessary, then what's possible, and suddenly you are doing the impossible."
   -St. Francis of Assisi

"Doing the best at this moment puts you in the best place for the next moment."
 -Oprah Winfrey

Love

"The best portion of a good man's life is his little, nameless, unremembered acts of kindness and love."
 -William Wordsworth

"To give pleasure to a single heart by a single kind act is better than a thousand head-bowings in prayer."
 -Saadi

"It is a good thing to be rich and a good thing to be strong, but it is a better thing to be loved by many friends."
 -Euripides

"A profound fact to reflect on, that every human creature is constituted to be that profound secret and mystery to each other."
    -Charles Dickens

"Those who bring sunshine to the lives of others cannot keep it from themselves."
    -Sir James Matthew Barrie

"A loving heart is the truest wisdom."
    -Charles Dickens

"I have learned that to be with those I like is enough."
    -Walt Whitman

Living in the moment

Openness

Value others

Engagement

If you are always looking ahead, expecting to find love or happiness around the next bend, in the years ahead, after you have reached some pinnacle of achievement or amassed some measure of wealth, you are missing the boat, missing out on countless opportunities every day to make your life richer. Happiness follows those who are mindful and appreciative of every step of the journey. Simple moments well-lived are the substance of a happy life.

CHAPTER TWELVE

THE SECRET CODE

he pieces of the amulet lay loosely assembled on my desk. HOPE, flanked by the open hand of blessing and the crescent moon, arced across the top. HA, in vertical letters, framed it left and right. In between was the faint outline of a bell.

Neither the public library nor the Internet had the information I had sought. Hundreds of books listed in the library's electronic file made reference to magical charms and amulets. But most were in fictional books for children. The serious works of scholars, historians or archaeologists were either on loan or missing.

Finding nothing, I turned again to the notes I had compiled since my first conversation with Sophie about the Code to Happiness.

I examined a set of notes I had scribbled following my meeting with Dr. Ortiz. The words "healthy lifestyle" were underlined in blue.

I thought about Ortiz while tapping the notebook against my knee. Not only had she allowed me access to her research, but I had felt my health and vigor returning since I had begun incorporating some of her tips into my daily regimen. I had heeded the doctor's advice – with the exception of recommended hours of rest – to the best of my ability. My diet was now more balanced, and I was also exercising regularly despite the hectic pace of recent weeks.

The doc's advice had helped to affect the most obvious changes in my life, but the advice I had received from the others I had encountered – Rube, Stover, Minitauer, and the rest – had had no less impact. Never before had I felt so alive. Never had each new day seemed filled with such wonder and promise.

Even the recent disappointments and turmoil – the layoff, Dad's struggle, Ellen's ongoing bouts with self-doubt and depression, and the daily ups and downs of family life – felt like threads of a tapestry that pulled my life together with meaning and purpose.

The layoff had compelled me to reassess not only my career, but how settled I had become in my life. Instead of nodding off into the dull sleep of complacency, I would pursue the opportunities that lay in front of me and pursue my passions.

I was particularly excited about the guidance provided by the HOPE acronym: find High impact areas to focus my energies on; identify the Opportunities in these areas, not the problems; then act on these opportunities from my Principles rather than from expediency, choosing to concentrate on Easy steps first in order to insure some initial success and build momentum towards longer term goals.

I turned on my computer and noticed I had received several new e-mails. One message was from Ellen. I opened that first.

> Dad:
>
>   Is it possible to live a life without regrets? Is it possible to die and never regret anything - not ONE thing?
>
>   I have had several conversations with an academic counselor, Mrs. Remcik, at the university. As you know, I don't usually warm quickly to people, particularly to "gurus" who think they can tell you what's wrong with your life and why you've made all the wrong choices. But - surprise, surprise! - I have found a kind of soul mate in her. We always start out talking about my academic and career interests. Invariably, however, our conversations slide into topics that draw me out of my shell of gloom. She taps me like an egg with questions, ever so softly, against the edge of the mixing bowl, until I break loose and drip, gooey and elastic with the messy truth, into the bottom of the bowl. Usually, it is for the better.
>
>   But our last meeting was very discomforting.
>
>   She volunteers for a support organization for people with cancer. Several times she has brought up stories of women who have died from cancer. The last one hit me very hard, however. A 67-year-old woman died last week.

She told Mrs. Remcik repeatedly about all the things she wished she had done. She was filled with regret she could not shake. If she had her life to do all over again, she would have attempted many of the things that had seemed too difficult or distant, things that she had scarcely allowed herself even to dream about.

I'm bothered by the fact that so many people die or grow old and regret the things they have done in life or the things they didn't do. They contemplate the million possibilities that passed them by like some speeding passenger train in the night. They wish, "If only I were aboard!"

I don't want this to happen to me. Anyway, Mrs. Remcik has tried to tell me how "lucky and talented" I am, like you and the others do. She reminds me that I am young and that countless possibilities are ahead of me. But her words – like your insistence that I am capable and successful – offer no comfort whatsoever. I know she means well, but I'm not looking for more advice, more "happy talk." I feel like life is passing me by…that I am simply wasting my time here at school...

All I really know is that I need to change my life. Wish I knew how...

Love,
Ellen

P.S. I forgot the real reason I started to send you this message. I'm coming home in two days. See ya. – E.S.

Gongs from the grandfather clock in the corner of my library interrupted my thoughts. I had a lot to do today. I printed out Ellen's letter, folded it and stuffed it in my jacket pocket.

Edmund J. Hoppe Hospital had begun to feel like a second home. I knew its hallways, waiting rooms, and cafeteria like the back of my hand. For better or for worse, its every activity left an imprint on my psyche. This time, I paid little attention to the building and its activities as I rushed through the corridors to see my father. I climbed the cascading steps from the hospital's entrance and headed to his room with a strange uneasiness.

"How's my father doing?" I asked the first nurse I recognized from the morning medical staff.

"He's comfortable," she said, nodding too long, touching my deepest fears.

He was sitting up when I entered his room. For as long as I could remember, his skin had had that leathery look of men of the earth who had spent too much time in the outdoors and paid without regret for their overdoses of wind and rain and cold and burning sunshine. Now, however, he just looked gray and weary.

He conjured a smile for me and grabbed my arm at the elbow.

"So, son," he finally said. "How will you describe me to your grandchildren?"

"I'll just let them take your picture and sit on your lap," I said without conviction. "They'll know for themselves."

Dad dug deep for a smile that said "Nice try."

The buoyant feeling I had had earlier evaporated like morning mist. We could find nothing else to say that hadn't already been said – in word or thought when our heads were clear and our hearts were not quite so leaden. I just leaned over and gave my dad a hug.

His left hand crossed his chest and tapped mine with all the strength he was able to muster.

The solemnity ended abruptly at the sound of hard footsteps and moving garments.

"There they are!" Dad whispered.

Ellen, Randy, and Eddie pushed into the room. For several long seconds, they stood awkwardly just inside the door. The sobriety of the hospital had stiffened their spirit, and they struggled for a grasp of proper decorum.

Dad's hand left mine and formed a fist. Its bones were gnarled like limbs of an old oak. But when that fist went up in triumphant salute, the ice broke. The kids tumbled in as if they were crashing an old friend's party. Eddie gave out an only slightly muffled "Hey, Gramps." Randy's giant hand seized his younger brother beneath the razor-line of a fresh haircut as if he were straddling a guitar neck. Eddie popped him in the solar plexus in retaliation. Even Ellen shook free of her gloom.

"I don't know who these guys are, Grandpa, but I think they're harmless," she said, kissing his cheek.

The change in Dad was profound and immediate, and given his weakened state, his smile seemed as boisterous as a belly laugh.

"Hey, Gramps," blurted Randy. "Look what Noodle Arm and I found in the closet underneath a pile of his moldy socks and gym shorts."

He held out an 8-by-10 inch photo of Dad and the two boys on the quarter-mile pier at St. Joseph, Michigan. Five-year-old Eddie stood between Dad and a scraggly-haired Randy, who was twice his size. Eddie's wide eyes and open mouth exclaimed his excitement as he held a yellow perch toward the camera. It was so fat that it looked like a comically crafted carving from the souvenir shop. The pier faded from the trio and converged with the lines of horizon, shoreline, and tree line into a single point beyond the pier and the riverbank. I remembered it well. I had been the guy behind the camera.

Dad's joy seemed to visibly fill his chest. He held the photo in his left hand, grabbed Ellen's arm with his right. She hugged him, smoothing the thin, unkempt gray hairs across his head.

"I bet that's still bigger than any perch Fuzz-Bass here has ever caught, right Grandpa?" said Eddie.

"One of the biggest I've ever seen Ed-boy," Dad purred. "One of the biggest ever."

Tears welled in the corners of my eyes.

Dad was in good company as I left him with the kids.

Still, he occupied my mind so much as I drove that I missed the turn for the museum. I turned on a one-way street a few blocks past and curled back along the boulevard.

Professor Stark sat amid a long table of artifacts. She was surrounded by pieces of unsolved mysteries. Shards of pottery. The tarnished, broken blade of a broad sword. A piece of yellow parchment with indecipherable hieroglyphics.

But Professor Stark's attention focused upon the piece of darkened metal in her hand.

"Mr. Socrates!" she exclaimed. "Just the man I hoped to run into today!"

"Hello, Professor Stark," I said. "What do you have there?"

"We may have hit the jackpot," she said, giving the fragment a final perusal before handing it to me. "Look what I found among our unsolved artifacts."

I looked at the new piece closely. It had the letter "P" inscribed on it. And it clearly matched the Hope amulet's style.

"Where did it come from?" I asked.

"That's the most puzzling thing about it. We have no documentation. No clue as to where it came from. Not a single identifier. If you hadn't played Peeping Tom the other night, I wouldn't have thought much of it."

"How do you think it got here?"

"No one on staff has a clue. I've been shaking the bushes all day. Let's see if the pieces match up."

I was even more excited to share my discovery now. I extracted a suede pouch with a brown leather drawstring from my jacket and set it on the table. Stark fell upon it like a cat on a mouse and took out the piece of the amulet with the "HA" inscribed on it.

We slid the pieces into position like kids with a giant jigsaw puzzle. They fit perfectly, spelling "HAP." I guess it wasn't "HA HA HA" after all, I thought to myself.

My heart raced as I walked back to the library and the unfinished work on my desk. Several note pages were fanned like playing cards. The "A" on my notes regarding *appreciation* had been overwritten so many times that the pen had cut through the paper. Abutting the "A" was the word PATIENCE that highlighted the notes from my meeting with Minitauer.

I tapped at the word with my right index finger as if sending a code, the letters of which I was myself uncertain. I noticed that it formed the letters "AP." A rush of adrenaline tingled through my spine.

I thought about my discovery of the HOPE acronym as I looked at the HAP parts of the amulet. I stared at my notes. I grabbed the notes from my meeting with Dr. Ortiz on healthy lifestyle. And circled the letter "H."

"H-A-P!" I said again, grabbing suddenly for the missing pages beneath the piles. "YOUTHFUL ENTHUSIASM" jumped out at me from the first page I resurrected. The ballpoint overstrikes on the letter "Y" caught the light and made the letter pulse as if it were neon.

A crumpled and dog-eared page stuck out from The Socrates Smith Notebook. I slid out the page with such vigor that the other papers on the desk rustled like leaves in an autumn breeze. The notes on the page conjured memories of my first meeting with Philip Stover. Pieces of our conversation flashed through my mind. I had summed up the lesson with the word, "passion." I studied the last two pages, added them to the others, then shuffled the pages and fanned them again. Then I took out one of the sheets and reinserted it like a novice gin rummy player hunting for a winning order from his hand.

"H-A-P-P-YOUTHFUL CURIOSITY," it read.

I grabbed the notebook, and listed the words again.

> *Healthy Lifestyle*
> *Appreciation*
> *Passion*
> *Patience*
> *Youthful Curiosity*

Then I boxed off the first letter of each line and grabbed another notebook, placing it face-down to isolate the letters further.

"Well, look at that!" I said aloud, falling down into the chair where Eddie had sat earlier.

"Would you look at that!"

> *H*
> *A*
> *P*
> *P*
> *Y*

I replayed the various conversations with my mentors that helped lead me to discover the secret Code to Happiness. Each conversation seemed to take on a deeper level of understanding in the light of the Code. I found my soul reaching to those architects of the Code and the maker of the amulet. I felt deeply connected to those who had brought me *hope*, taught me about *love*, and now, finally, anchored the Code's spirit in the word *happy*.

I suddenly felt alone. And I was. Where had all my family gone? I had become so absorbed in the Code that I had not sensed the rare silence that had allowed me to work uninterrupted, had carried me to the Code's conclusion.

But I was alone in another sense as well – alone in my discovery of the Code and its power. I wanted to share it, spread it, offer it as a cure to the ailments of the world, and use it as a tonic to bring happiness to the multitudes. But I knew I could not…at least not so simply, not without passing along its lessons.

And would that – even then – be enough to bring others happiness?

Only if they repeated those lessons and became disciples. They had to let the spirit of the Code take hold of their soul. They had to mix its recipe, day after day after day so that it became a way of life. An approach to life which I now understood was the key to happiness. Happiness wasn't something to possess. It was, rather, a consequence of leading a good life. The Code, like the amulet, was valuable only in the direction it offered, not in its possession as a material object.

I itched to spill this great jar of delight out on the kitchen table for all to taste and eat and thrive upon.

The house shuddered, the convulsion of a door opening and a house filling with air and the flesh and spirit that make a house a home. The Smith family was back. Bags of groceries rustled. Eddie and Randy barked with their relentless banter.

Carrie queried Ellen about school as they stocked the refrigerator and pantry. How different their discussion was from the ones that I had with Ellen. Theirs was filled with lively descriptions of campus, concerts, and clothing stores, while ours lately had been laden with her angst.

Meanwhile, the boys toted what seemed an endless stream of grocery sacks from car to kitchen. Eddie twanged guitar-like tones reminiscent of one of the songs that Randy had recently written. Randy roared back with the melody, plopping bags of groceries on the counter and banging out a drum roll on the table as he pivoted and bolted back through the door for the final load of groceries. I felt like a theater patron, enjoying a good family comedy.

Carrie stacked several jars of spaghetti sauce and pasta in the pantry and grabbed an envelope from the counter.

"It looks like you got your check from Stover," she said, tapping my forehead with the envelope and kissing me like a schoolgirl. I hugged her and kissed her back. Ellen smiled and shook her head at the antics of a married couple still hungry for love and each other's company and the wild roller-coaster of family life.

"And what, pray tell, did you do today?" asked Carrie.

"Not much. Except for unlocking a secret Code," I said, feeling like a soaring hawk seeing the world and all its beauty anew.

Carrie gave me a puzzling look, but before she could ask me what I meant, the phone rang. She answered it, still looking at me with curiosity written all over her face.

"Yes. Yes," she said. "I'll get him."

Something in her tone put a damper on the boys' music, froze Ellen in her tracks.

Carrie's expression changed. She bit her bottom lip as she handed me the phone.

My response was one word, "Yes," spoken four times and "Thank you," spoken once when we were finished. It was all the conversation I could muster. I hung up the phone and gathered strength from a deep reservoir I rarely knew even existed.

The chill of loss frosted the air, crawled up my back like a winter wind. The four laughing faces before me had turned ashen. The words fell out of my mouth like nails from a carpenter's lips.

"Dad's gone."

CHAPTER THIRTEEN

THE HAPPIEST PERSON
IN THE WORLD

The envelope lay, flap open, on the table. "Dad," it read, in Ellen's handwriting.

"Sometime, Dad, when I'm back at school…read this," Ellen had said two days after the funeral. She had held the envelope in two hands, guarding its contents even as she yielded it. "But please, not now."

And so I had honored her wish, setting the envelope first on my dresser, later in my library, isolating it from mail and notebooks and the piles of unfinished readings. Ellen had gone back to school, and, perhaps out of respect, I waited still.

I looked at the envelope on my desk daily, trying to hold my curiosity at bay as I waited for a chime in my mind to signal "ready."

It had more breathing room in the library – particularly since I had begun reading in the living room, where my presence would not crowd it.

But the time to open it was close at hand. I tapped its corner on the hardwood of the DΣLPHI table and set it down again. I slid it off to the side, out of the reach of the faint ring my coffee mug had left, beyond the boundary of the newspaper that I turned to today with the warm pleasure of one who has unearthed a favorite shirt or pair of shoes long believed lost.

It felt good to settle in for coffee again at the DΣLPHI Café. I had stopped in twice since Dad's passing. Each time, it had worn a respectfully somber air, as if even everyday commerce had paused to pay homage to Dad. Patrons came through the DΣLPHI doors at what I guessed to be one-third their normal number. I had expected George to show some sign of anxiety at the poor turnout, but with Sophie at her post again and his financing clear for his new restaurant venture, not even the quiet cash register gave George cause for alarm.

*N*o man is an island unto himself.
        Each is a piece of the continent, a part of the main.

John Donne's words had played in my mind during Dad's funeral service as that long retinue of folks who counted themselves among Abraham Smith's friends, family, and glad-I-knew-him acquaintances filed past the coffin, paying their respects.

Ira Rosenstein, Dad's frequent angling pal in his later years, led the way with his wife and two grown sons. Rose Watson, who had worked with Dad for 20 years and had recently lost her husband to a long illness, wiped tears from her eyes under the protective arm of her son, a handsome black man, lean and athletic, who stood out like a monument in the crowd. Among the mourners, too, was Mr. Kim, my neighbor for the past 15 years, whose children had hung around Dad whenever we sat in the yard as if he were Santa Claus and the Easter Bunny wrapped into one.

My personal connection with my father, the way I had framed my memory of him as parent, provider, and constant companion in my youth, had skewed my view of him. The mix of age, profession, race, and creed there in solemn procession at the church told a story of a life larger than I had taken time to appreciate. A marvelous potpourri of humanity had gathered to pay homage to a man whose humble greatness I was still coming to understand. Dad was connected to them all, as Donne had declared. As they were to Dad. As we, the Smith family, were now to them.

I had spoken of this theme in my eulogy, borrowing from my memories of a day spent among the giant redwood trees of California. Walking among these giants had been like strolling through a living temple, thousands of years old and destined to stand for endless millennia. The trees were towering and immense, some scarred from forest fires that had not only failed to destroy them but had helped their seeds to germinate so that more of these mighty creatures might grow. I admired the trees' thick bark and sculpted burls. I thought about how different the world had been at their birth and how different it would be hundreds of years from now.

But, at the point where I was feeling so small as to be virtually microscopic, I came upon a guidepost that explained what I found to be the most fascinating fact of all about these monuments to the divine. What made the giant redwood so strong and able to withstand countless assaults from wind and storm and fire was their root system. The clusters of giants, hundreds of feet tall, grew so close that they became interconnected. Even trees finally felled by Nature sometimes survived long after their tumble. They were part of a family whose roots commingled. The redwoods were strong in themselves, but far stronger together.

And here in the middle of my father's church, a different type of community mingled its roots and shared the nourishment he had given to them and they to him.

The all-embracing ecumenism of my father's life showed itself again as his boyhood friend, Don Linder, now Rabbi Linder, took the pulpit. The rabbi's gray beard was long and full, and, though he moved with the deliberation of a man carrying the common debilities of a life more than seven decades full, his eyes were as bright as a child's.

The Rabbi first related a story about an experience he and my father had shared as young boys. They had "borrowed" a neighbor's canoe during the high waters of spring on the creek that flowed through their town. They were caught in the current and carried downstream. The canoe trapped them in a nest of tree limbs, white with the wash of the rushing stream. And while the canoe did not make it, the boys, bruised and waterlogged, most fortunately did.

Lucky to have come away with their lives, he recalled how both he and his friend Abe had carried the vivid memory like a precious family memento. In sharing their plight and helping to ensure each other's survival, they had forged a bond that had kept their friendship alive, even during the decades when continents, vocations, and families separated them.

The congregation seemed to be lifted by the rabbi's message, as much a reflection of his friend's philosophy as of his own spiritual convictions.

"We fear age because we fail to understand life," he said. "We view our stay on earth as a matter of economics, hoping to get maximum mileage out of the vehicle of our body. Life, in this view, is something we consume.

"In Abraham Smith's world, a different view prevailed. His life was an accumulation of experience and well-sorted wisdom. As his body aged, his spirit remained youthful, his enthusiasm and curiosity more insatiable with each passing year.

"Even in his death, we can still feel his spirit alive among us. Listen closely and you can hear his voice, whether it be a whisper or his boisterous cry, exhorting you to live life to the fullest, to take a great bite out of each day, taking strength and wisdom from both the sweet and the bitter bites.

"Knowing Abraham Smith as long and as intimately as I have, I would not call him a perfect man. And I am sure that he, lying in his casket, would have to say the same about me. True, he had traits that stood out at times like gems, large and perfectly cut, impeccably placed. But it wasn't perfection that we needed, and it wasn't perfection that we loved. It was the man himself, his rough-hewn manner, his transparent goodness, and a love of life that sometimes barged right through your door like a long lost friend, lifting you from your television and the boredom you didn't even realize had taken hold.

"No, Abe was not perfect. But I learned a simple truth from a teacher of mine long ago: God does not demand perfection. He prefers goodness. And Abraham Smith's goodness remains alive and well and is flowing today through each of us who knew him."

And as I looked around the church, I recognized another simple truth. The love my father had brought to his family and his friends was what linked us all, more celebrants than mourners, like the interconnected roots of those ancient redwoods.

Having unlocked the Code to Happiness, I found myself noticing its themes and lessons in everything and everyone.

In remembering my dad, I knew that he had given me many gifts, including, in his last days, the gift of love and appreciation that now swelled my heart with understanding in ways that my mind could once only abstractly understand. The Code helped me understand that happiness starts with the small seed of hope, and my dad had spent a lifetime rejuvenating that hope with his optimism, good nature, and appreciation for whatever experiences life threw his way. Other aspects of the Code, once too subtle to notice, now helped guide my days towards fulfillment and satisfaction.

Solving the Code had, however, brought little sense of individual accomplishment, for I knew I was neither an accomplished explorer nor clever detective. I had only found what I had been led to, like a horse led to water. My sole accomplishment had been in deciding to drink. But weren't we all, at one time or another, fed the precepts of the Code: to have faith and hope; to love; to protect our health; to appreciate what we have; to exercise patience and let things come to fruition; to retain the curiosity of youth, and to pursue our passions in life? Isn't it ironic, I thought, that we too often fail to digest the simple lessons needed for the one thing the soul craves most – happiness?

If the secrets from the DΣLPHI Café had taught me anything, it was that the answers to our deepest desires were in our midst.

The Code and Dad's last days would forever be linked in my memory. Of that, I was certain.

But one moment stood out among all others.

Before the funeral, I was so surprised by Ellen's request to speak that I fumbled with words of encouragement.

As she stepped to the pulpit following my eulogy, I was even more surprised. Was this the same young woman whom I had seen so often wallowing in despair, turning triumph into defeat with relentless consistency? Was this the same woman who, only days earlier, had judged academic life – life in general – to be "so meaningless"?

What a wonderful transformation had taken place in those hours following her grandfather's passing! Tears of loss flowed freely as she recalled her grandfather's life and what he had meant to her, to her brothers, and to those who had been blessed with his acquaintance. But no shroud of grief could cover the beauty we witnessed as her voice rose with a newfound confidence, like sails full with the wind of hope.

Something had lifted a burden from my daughter's soul. Her voice had rung bold and brilliant, like a choir in triumphant song.

"....Grandpa helped me understand that I had been letting the small clouds of my little problems eclipse the golden sun of my life...For my grandfather, Abraham Smith, the stars of hope and love and appreciation blazed brightly until his final hour. His celebration of life is a call to me, to all of us, to live a life that matters."

Tears welled up in my eyes. I missed my dad, but he had given my daughter the greatest of gifts in his passing.

Professor Stark had cast two molds of the Hope amulet. One of them, with inset zircons and other artificial gems, hung on the wall over the desk in my library. Every day I recalled those who had guided me to unlock the Code to Happiness and to ponder its lessons.

Twice already, I had stopped at the museum to gaze upon the original. Professor Stark had difficulty winning favor for the idea of a permanent display for the amulet. Several members of the museum board challenged the authenticity of the Hope amulet, and two others argued that the entire legend of the amulet was a bad hoax.

Six days after unlocking the Code, the argument became moot. I had met Professor Stark at the museum to share the Code to Happiness with her. I was in the middle of explaining my belief that the letters HAP was really short for HAPPY, but we were missing the final piece of the amulet. I was planning to ask Sophie if she knew where we might find it.

"Who is this Sophie?"

"She's an ora…She's an unusual woman. And I don't know quite how to describe her without convincing you that both Sophie and I are two jacks shy of a full deck."

"Speak for yourself, partner. I'll take my own chances." Sophie's voice cut brazenly through the heavy quiet of the museum, sweeping the must and dust of the back room into sudden flight. A fresh breeze seemed to have followed her in. She wore the everyday outfit of the DƩLPHI.

"Professor Stark, meet Sophie," I said.

"Hello, Ms. Sophie," said the professor, puzzled and off-balance with Sophie's sudden appearance. "Are you an archaeologist?"

"Sorry, Professor Stark," said Sophie. "I dig up a lot of things going on around town, but I'm not exactly an archaeologist."

"What do you do?" asked the professor.

"Well, it seems that most of the time I clean up this guy's coffee puddles at the DƩLPHI Café downtown."

"You're a…waitress, then?"

"Professor Stark, the care and attention of coffee-loving Americans is a most noble profession, I assure you. I serve pipe welders, painters, physicians and folks representing a couple hundred other career paths that don't start with "P" six days a week, 52 weeks a year. OK, 51-1/2 weeks this year. You leave town for two days, and they send the FBI out after you."

She was at it again. Professor Stark was helpless against the torrent of Sophie. "Don't mind her, Professor," I said. "She's too difficult to explain and even harder to contain."

Professor Stark pushed between us as Sophie pulled out the white bag and slid out its contents. Sophie showed us a new piece of the amulet. It contained the letters "PY."

Stark swept up the arcing segments and fit them against the pieces set on the table.

I slid crumpled sheets of tissue beneath three of the pieces to align their broken edges. The amulet took on congruous form and a shadowy elegance.

"Now watch this," said Sophie.

She bent the piece slowly in the light. We tapped the pieces into place, lining up the broken edges as best we could. When we had completed the task to our satisfaction, we stared at our re-creation.

And then I saw it. Its message was as simple as the first word on a birthday greeting card. It read:

HAPPY

Professor Stark and I were delighted. We drank a toast together with the only thing available: our soft drinks. Sophie seemed genuinely pleased as well. I had never seen her wearing such a big smile.

We finally parted company with Professor Stark, promising to keep the pieces to the amulet that now, as finally reconstructed, spelled both HOPE and HAPPY, in a safe place overnight and then locked in the museum vault the following day until a decision was made about what to do with it.

And then, the next day, the amulet disappeared.

Professor Stark was mortified.

Sophie was, hmmm, rather quiet on the subject.

I…well, let's just say I was not that surprised.

I grew even fonder of the replica in my library after the disappearance of the original charm. Each member of the family had caught me musing over it and had asked about its significance.

Eddie called it "Cool!" on his way out the door to play basketball at the recreation center.

Randy seemed to pay scant attention to my capsule explanation of the amulet, but the following day he surprised me with a striking pencil sketch of the charm that over time I would prize as much as the replica.

Carrie had listened patiently as I explained the elements of the Code. When I came to appreciation, and explained its relationship to love, I leaned over and hugged her. I felt closer to my family than ever before. Yet whenever an opportunity to relate my local odyssey appeared, they became vaguely disinterested. When I opened my mouth to attempt an explanation for those I wanted most to share it with, my words tripped out in what must have sounded like simple terms of endearment and hugs and pats on the back.

Only Ellen gave a hint of recognition.

She had come to say good-bye before heading back to school and had caught me in one of my frequent reveries on some piece of the Code or the mentors who had brought it to life for me. Before I could rise, she froze me with a questioning look. Her eyes shuffled between the wall ornament and my face. I could see questions formulating behind her now shining eyes as she wondered what revelations lay behind the plaster replica of the Hope amulet.

But a smile formed, and the kind of peace I had thought would always remain foreign to her spread across her face and radiated from her like the warmth of a glowing hearth. Feeling a parent's sense of relief for a child who seemed poised for success, my heart soared.

I tapped the corner of the envelope on the table for what must have been the twentieth time that day. Her last words echoed in my mind again.

"Sometime, Dad, when I'm back at school…read this."

Now was the time.

She had handed me the envelope before pulling away in her car, an old clunker that I had helped her purchase late last year. I opened it and saw her recent e-mail regarding the possibility of living life without regrets. On the back of the page was a note. I recognized the handwriting. It was my father's. I began to read.

Dear Ellie,

Your Dad left this letter on my bed today when he was at the hospital. I presume he meant to answer your e-mail, but left it behind accidentally.

I hope you forgive a dying man for deciding to poke his pointy nose into this matter, but I have a few words to say to my granddaughter on the subject of regrets.

You asked if it is possible to live a life without them. I don't know if anyone goes through life without any regrets, but somewhere along the line, it dawns on many of us greybeards that regrets are pointless. What's done is done. Furthermore, I would venture a guess that many folks come to realize – and appreciate – the stubborn truth that many of their worst experiences happened for the better. Getting kicked in the tail made them stronger or smarter. Or, more importantly, nicer. Having bad times made them appreciate the good times more, placed things in perspective, or just plain steered them onto a better road.

Hell, the truth is, Ellie, all those times, good and bad, gave them a life. And saying good-bye to regrets, leaving that old baggage behind, is the best way to make life big and beautiful.

Things don't always go the way we would like them to. But I can't emphasize enough the importance of not giving up your dreams - even when disappointments come or circumstances dictate that we put them on hold. These potholes along life's road are filled with lessons that make the journey, wherever it takes us, worthwhile.

As for a role model, your father is probably as good as they get. Yes, I know that he is a little odd and academic, but he is full of hope and love, high on ideas, and appreciates things with the best of us old codgers. He wasn't always this way. Somewhere, somehow he made the right turn.

Seeing the world fresh, keeping the mind young, being absorbed with the wonders around us – these are the only ways I know of to stay energetic, enthusiastic, and happy. Soaking up what is happening right now is the first step. You can't wait for happiness to come "when I earn a ton of money" or "achieve XYZ" or marry Mr. Perfect. It don't work that way, Miss Ellie.

I'm getting a little tired now, granddaughter. Only have time for one more word on regrets: they are @#$%! Like I said: What's done is done. Time to move on. Better to ask: What can I learn from the past? What can I do about tomorrow? And, most importantly, what do I have to be thankful for right now?

Mistakes? Yep. I made 'em. But, heck, some of those mistakes turned into the best things in my whole life.

Hope this helps.
I love you,
Grandpa Abe

"Look who's deep in thought."

It was Sophie.

"So, what's on your mind?" she asked.

"Well, let's see…That my father was a great man. That the secret Code to Happiness is real, but you have to want it and take it to heart and make its truths your own before it will change your life. And you have to rekindle that quest for the Code each and every day. That's the path to the good life that men and women really want, a life filled with joy and pleasure and happiness.

"That doesn't mean that you won't have moments of sadness or disappointment," I continued. "They are part of life. Part of being human. If we hide from them or try to discard them like unwanted rubbish, we will cast out part of our humanity with them and thus lose some of our capacity for joy."

I waited for a wisecrack or some other witticism. None came. Sophie smiled, sat down, and poured me another cup of George's special for the day.

"You remind me of another pilgrim, a man who went searching for the Code to Happiness, oh, about 30 years ago," she said.

"Who was that?"

"It was a fellow by the name of Abraham. Abraham Smith."

She stood up and disappeared behind the DΣLPHI counter.

I was speechless.

From the doorway behind the counter, Sophie's head appeared. Joy took off like a rocket, slow and burning, exploding within me in a burst of pyrotechnics.

Sophie stepped to the counter and reached toward a vase of roses, my gift to her that morning. Deftly, she plucked one from the bunch, broke its stem and set it behind her ear.

She winked at me.

My smile stretched across the room. My heart grew too large for my chest.

For at that moment, I was, indeed, the happiest person in the world.

The End